AI FOR BEGINNERS

GRASP GENERATIVE AI AND MACHINE LEARNING,
ADVANCE YOUR CAREER, AND EXPLORE THE ETHICAL
IMPLICATIONS OF ARTIFICIAL INTELLIGENCE

IN JUST 31 DAYS

TINA E BRADLEY

© 2024 **Tina E. Bradley**. All rights reserved.

No part of this book may be copied, reproduced, stored, or distributed in any form—whether electronic, mechanical, photocopying, recording or otherwise—without prior **written permission from the author or publisher**, except in cases of brief quotations for reviews or educational purposes as permitted by law.

This book is **licensed for personal use only**. It may not be resold, shared, or uploaded to any website, file-sharing platform, or database without authorization. Unauthorized reproduction or distribution of this work is **a violation of copyright law** and may result in **legal action**.

All trademarks, product names, and company names mentioned in this book are the property of their respective owners. Their inclusion does not imply endorsement or affiliation.

The content of this book is provided **"as is"** without warranties of any kind, express or implied. The author and publisher are not responsible for any errors, omissions, or outcomes resulting from the use of this material.

For permissions, inquiries, or rights requests, please contact:

SereneWisdom Works

https://www.serenewisdomworks.com

Disclaimer Notice:

This book contains links to external websites, including YouTube videos, blogs, and other resources provided for informational and educational purposes. The author and publisher do not own or control these external sites and are not responsible for their accuracy, availability, or content. Inclusion of these links does not imply endorsement. Readers should independently verify the accuracy and relevance of external resources, as their availability may change without notice.

This book is provided **"as is"** without warranties of any kind, express or implied. The author does not provide legal, financial, medical, or professional advice. The content is based on sources believed to be reliable, but no guarantee is made regarding its completeness or accuracy.

Additionally, the **practice exercises, tutorials, and step-by-step guides** reflect tools and workflows available at the time of publication. Due to the rapid advancement of **Artificial Intelligence and related technologies**, some information may become outdated. Readers should consult updated documentation or professional guidance for the latest tools and techniques.

The author and publisher are not liable for any errors, omissions, or consequences arising from the use of this material. Readers are encouraged to exercise discretion and conduct their own research when applying the information in this book.

CONTENTS

Introduction   vii

1. BUILDING THE FOUNDATIONS OF AI: FROM BASICS TO KEY CONCEPTS   1
   Simplifying AI: Key Terms and Concepts Explained   1
   From Algorithms to Zettabytes: A Visual Dictionary of AI   3
   Generative AI: Innovating Through Creation   4
   Machine Learning vs. AI: Understanding the Distinctions   8
   Deciphering Neural Networks   12
   NLP Explained: How Machines Understand Us   15
   Knowledge Check: Chapter 1   18

2. RELIABLE AI RESOURCES FOR BEGINNERS   19
   Curating Your AI Learning Toolkit: Top Resources   19
   Online Platforms for AI Learning: What to Choose and Why   21
   Essential Books and Journals on AI for Beginners   23
   Following the Right Experts: Blogs and Social Media to Watch   26
   Leveraging University and Online Course Resources   28
   Knowledge Check: Chapter 2   31

3. THE SUBTLE INTELLIGENCE POWERING YOUR WORLD   33
   Smart Home Devices: Enhancing Your Living Space with AI   33
   Personal Finance and AI: Budgeting and Investment Tools   36
   AI-Powered Apps to Keep You Healthy   38
   Entertainment and AI: How Algorithms Influence What You Watch and Listen To   40
   AI in Personal Organization and Productivity Tools   42
   Knowledge Check: Chapter 3   44

4. UTILIZING AI IN YOUR CAREER 45
　How AI is Shaking Up Marketing 45
　AI for Project Managers: Enhancing Decision-Making and Efficiency 48
　The Role of AI in Data-Driven Decision Making 50
　Enhancing Customer Service with AI Technologies 53
　AI and HR: Recruiting and Onboarding Innovations 58
　Knowledge Check: Chapter 4 62

5. STAYING CURRENT WITH AI TRENDS 65
　Tracking AI Innovations: Key Trends to Watch 65
　Participating in AI Conferences and Webinars 67
　Reading Scientific Papers on AI: A Beginner's Approach 69
　The Future of AI: Predictions and Preparations 73
　Knowledge Check: Chapter 5 78

6. HANDS-ON AI PROJECTS 79
　Building Your First Chatbot 80
　Creating a Simple Recommender System 82
　Introduction to Using AI for Basic Image Recognition 83
　Unleashing AI in Music and Social Media 86
　Analyzing Social Media Sentiments with AI 88
　Knowledge Check: Chapter 6 92

7. ETHICAL AI USE AND CONSIDERATIONS 93
　Understanding AI Bias and How to Mitigate It 94
　Privacy Concerns with AI Technologies 96
　The Societal Impact of AI: A Balanced View 98
　Developing Transparent AI Systems 101
　Ethical AI Design and Development Practices 103
　Knowledge Check: Chapter 7 107

8. CAREER PATHS IN AI 109
　Exploring AI Job Roles and Required Skills 109
　How to Transition to a Career in AI 112
　Skills Development: From Novice to AI Expert 113
　Networking and Building Professional Relationships in AI 115
　The Role of Certifications and Advanced Education in AI Careers 117
　Knowledge Check: Chapter 8 121

9. ADVANCED BEGINNER CHALLENGES AND PROJECTS	123
Advanced Project: Crafting a Simple AI Model with Python	123
Integrating AI with Visualization Tools	126
Troubleshooting Common AI Project Challenges	128
Keeping Your AI Knowledge and Skills Future-Proof	132
Knowledge Check: Chapter 9	138
10. BONUS CHAPTER: AI AND DIGITAL AFTERLIFE	139
What Happens to Our Digital Selves After We're Gone?	139
The Rise of Digital Afterlife: From Memories to Avatars	140
The Cultural Shift: Redefining Death, Memory, and Legacy	142
The Psychological Impact: Does Digital Immortality Change Grieving?	143
Exploring the Future of Digital Immortality	144
Privacy After Death: Protecting Loved Ones	149
Conclusion	155
11. 31-DAY JOURNEY: YOUR AI LEARNING PLAN	161
Additional Resources	163
Answer Key to Knowledge Check	165
References	169

INTRODUCTION

Artificial Intelligence (AI) is everywhere—whether it's Netflix suggesting your next binge-worthy show or your phone instantly recognizing your face. It's changing the way we live, work, and interact with technology, and honestly, it's happening fast.

I'm Tina E. Bradley, the founder of Serene Wisdom Works, a publishing company focused on making complex topics, like AI, easy to understand. As an IT specialist with a background in database administration and scripting, I've spent my career translating technical jargon into something people can actually use. This book is a reflection of that passion—because learning technology shouldn't feel like decoding an alien language.

Maybe you're a student stepping into a tech-driven world, a professional looking to stay ahead of the game, or just someone curious about AI. No matter where you're coming from, this book is for you. Together, we'll break down AI step by step, build a strong foundation, and gradually explore hands-on applications that will help you put AI to work in real life.

What's Inside This Book?

This isn't just a guide to AI—it's your personalized toolkit for navigating and leveraging this transformative technology. Along the way, you'll find:

- **A 31-Day Plan** to guide your learning step by step, helping you gain confidence and momentum.
- A downloadable **AI Essentials Toolkit** packed with resources, including:
  - A glossary of essential AI terms for quick reference.
  - Practice exercises to help you apply what you learn.
  - A curated list of beginner-friendly courses to expand your expertise.
- Interactive exercises, real-world examples, and ethical discussions that ensure you understand the implications and responsibilities of using AI effectively.
- A **Free Bonus Chapter** exploring how AI intersects with topics you may not expect, like the concept of a digital afterlife, offering an intriguing glimpse into the future of AI.

AI isn't just about robots or high-tech labs—it's shaping everything from social media to finance to how we shop online. Knowing how it works isn't just useful—it's becoming essential. That's why my goal is to make AI feel approachable, understandable, and—most importantly—practical.

Why Ethics Matter

AI is powerful, but like any powerful tool, it comes with responsibilities. Who gets to decide how AI is used? How do we prevent bias and protect privacy? Throughout this book, we'll dive into these important conversations to ensure that AI serves people—not the other way around.

Your Journey Begins Now

As you turn the pages, you'll discover how AI can help you solve problems, create opportunities, and even spark innovation. This book isn't just about keeping up with AI—it's about using it to your advantage. So, let's explore, learn, and build a future where you're not just keeping up with AI—you're leading with it.

1

BUILDING THE FOUNDATIONS OF AI: FROM BASICS TO KEY CONCEPTS

Ever heard people throw around terms like *machine learning*, *algorithms*, or *data mining* and felt completely lost? You're not alone! AI (Artificial Intelligence) is becoming a huge part of our daily lives, but the way it's explained often sounds more complicated than it needs to be.

This chapter is here to change that. We're going to break these terms down in a way that actually makes sense—without all the unnecessary jargon. By the end, you'll not only understand these concepts but also see how they're shaping the world around you.

SIMPLIFYING AI: KEY TERMS AND CONCEPTS EXPLAINED

At its core, AI is just about making machines *smart*. But before we dive deeper, let's get comfortable with a few key terms that will pop up throughout this book. We'll explain them in everyday language and connect them to things you already use.

Artificial Intelligence (AI): Artificial Intelligence (AI) is the science of making machines intelligent. It enables machines to perform tasks that usually require human effort, such as speech recognition, decision-making, and language translation. For example, when machines suggest the best route to work or recommend a movie, that's AI at work. We use this technology every day on our mobile devices.

Algorithms: An algorithm is a set of instructions similar to a recipe for solving problems. As a cookbook guides you in baking, an algorithm directs a computer to process information and reach a solution. For instance, Google Maps uses algorithms to find optimal routes, while Netflix suggests shows based on your viewing history.

Machine Learning: Machine Learning, a branch of AI, enables computers to learn from data rather than being manually programmed. For example, it automatically filters spam in emails, recommends products on shopping sites, and selects social media posts for you first.

Deep Learning: A machine learning technique using neural networks that mimic brain neurons. Each network component processes a small data segment, and together they produce the outcome.

Virtual assistants like Siri and Alexa process your voice by breaking it down into manageable parts. When you issue a command, the microphone captures it, and the system sequentially works to interpret your words. This efficient process allows the assistant to understand and respond appropriately, creating the impression that they get it.

Data Mining: Picture yourself as a detective sifting through clues to solve a mystery. Data mining is similar; it involves examining large amounts of data to find valuable patterns for decision-making. For example, retailers use data mining to analyze customer buying patterns, helping them optimize their inventories based on seasonal demand.

These terms reveal AI's power to transform industries and enhance daily life. Whether it's the route you take to work, the movies you watch, or how businesses understand customer behavior, AI is making things smarter, faster, and more personalized.

By the end of this section, you should feel more comfortable with these terms and understand their connection to technology and daily tasks. This knowledge underpins advanced AI operations and applications, which we will explore further in this book.

FROM ALGORITHMS TO ZETTABYTES: A VISUAL DICTIONARY OF AI

Ever tried reading foreign street signs? That's what AI can feel like without familiarity with the jargon. But don't worry! This visual dictionary is your guide, breaking down AI terms clearly.

This isn't just a boring glossary of definitions. Each entry comes with extra layers to help you get the concepts:

- **Visual Aids:** Diagrams and infographics make tricky ideas easier to understand. Imagine seeing a simple illustration showing how artificial neurons connect—like the human brain at work.
  - **QR Codes:** Need a deeper dive? Scan the QR codes to check out extra resources like articles, videos, and interactive tutorials that bring AI concepts to life.
  - **Expert Quotes:** Alongside each definition, you'll find real-world examples and quotes from AI pros who work in the field. They'll help connect the dots between theory and practice.

The goal here isn't just to memorize definitions—it's to *understand* them practically and helpfully. Whether you're brushing up on AI basics or tackling new concepts, this dictionary will make sure you're never stuck guessing. By the time you're done, you'll feel more confident using AI in your personal and professional life.

Click the link or scan the QR code to download AI Essentials: Tools, Exercises, and Resources.

AI Essentials: Tools, Exercises, and Resources

GENERATIVE AI: INNOVATING THROUGH CREATION

Imagine an AI that doesn't just analyze data—it creates something new. That's the magic of Generative AI! Whether writing text, composing music, designing images, or even generating videos, this technology reshapes how we interact with machines.

1. What Exactly is Generative AI?

- **Definition**: Generative AI is a type of machine learning that recognizes patterns rather than just identifying them. It learns from existing data and then creates new content that looks, sounds, or feels similar.
- **How it differs**: Most AI systems analyze and predict based on what already exists. Generative AI, on the other hand, takes that knowledge and turns it into something fresh—like writing a new song, painting a digital masterpiece, or even generating lifelike human faces that don't belong to real people.
- **Types of Data Generated**:
    - **Text** (articles, stories, scripts)
    - **Images** (artwork, photorealistic pictures)
    - **Audio** (music, speech)
    - **Videos** (animations, realistic videos)

2. How Generative AI Works

So, how does Generative AI create new content? It all comes down to learning patterns from tons of data and using that knowledge to generate something fresh. There are a few main ways AI pulls this off:

- **Generative Adversarial Networks (GANs)**:

Think of GANs as a creative competition between two AI models:

- **The Generator**: This AI tries to create new content—like an image or a song—that looks like the real deal.
    - **The Discriminator**: This AI plays the critic's role, judging whether the content is authentic or fake.
    - They improve by challenging each other: the Generator creates more realistic content while the Discriminator sharpens its flaw detection. This dynamic makes the AI's creations increasingly convincing!
- **Variational Autoencoders (VAEs)**:
    - Imagine shrinking a 3D object into a 2D image while keeping its essential details. That's what VAEs do!
    - They compress data into a smaller, more straightforward format and then use that information to generate something similar to the original.
    - This method is super helpful in creating new content that stays true to the patterns of the original data.
- **Transformer Models**:
    - Like GPT (Generative Pre-trained Transformers), transformers are the masterminds behind AI-generated text.
    - Instead of looking at words one by one, these models consider the entire context to predict the next word in a sentence, making the writing flow naturally.
    - This is why chatbots, virtual assistants, and AI-generated articles sound more human-like than ever!

3. Real-world applications of Generative AI

Generative AI isn't just incredible—it's changing the game in multiple industries, making everything from art to healthcare more innovative, faster, and creative. Here's a look at how AI is shaking things up:

- **Art and Design**:
    - AI-generated artwork is taking the creative world by storm! Artists use AI to explore new styles, patterns, and techniques they wouldn't have thought of independently.
    - Programs like DALL·E let anyone (even those who can't draw a stick figure) create stunning visuals by describing them in words.
- **Writing and Text Generation**:
    - Do you need an article, a blog post, or a chatbot dialogue? AI tools like GPT-4 can create human-like text in seconds.
    - **Example:** Jasper AI helps businesses write blog posts, ad copy, and social media content—feed it a few prompts, and it does the heavy lifting!
- **Music and Audio Creation**:
    - Whether you're making beats or composing orchestral scores, AI-powered music tools like Amper Music and Google's Magenta help musicians create original sounds.
    - **Example:** You can input a mood or style, and the AI will generate a custom piece of music in that genre.
- **Video Game Development**:
    - AI is making game development more straightforward and immersive through procedural generation, which allows it to create entire levels, landscapes, or characters independently.
    - **Example:** AI-generated landscapes and character designs, as seen in games like *No Man's Sky*.
- **Healthcare**:
    - Generative AI is making breakthroughs in healthcare by creating synthetic medical data (like MRI scans) to train

doctors and AI models without exposing accurate patient data. This not only preserves privacy but also helps improve medical research and diagnostics.

4. The Benefits of Generative AI

Generative AI isn't just a cool tech trend—it's a **game-changer** for creativity, productivity, and personalization. Here's how it's making life easier and more innovative across different fields:

- **Efficiency**: AI can generate high-quality content quickly, reducing the time needed to produce text, music, or images.
- **Creative Collaboration**: AI is an innovative partner, helping writers, artists, and musicians generate new ideas.
- **Personalization**: Notice how Netflix suggests shows and Spotify curates playlists? That's generative AI customizing content to your tastes—ads, product recommendations, or entertainment.
- **Cost-Effective Content Creation**: Businesses can save time and money by using AI to automatically generate marketing materials, social media content, and product descriptions, resulting in more output and less manual effort.

5. Challenges and Ethical Considerations

Generative AI is exciting, but it has challenges and ethical dilemmas. As this technology continues to evolve, we need to address some big questions:

- **Data Privacy**: AI models learn from large datasets, which may include personal information. The main concern is ensuring private data isn't misused or leaked. Responsible AI development must prioritize data security and user privacy.
- **Plagiarism and Ownership**: If an AI writes a novel or paints a digital masterpiece, who gets the credit—the person who gave the prompt or the company that built the AI? In creative

industries like art, writing, and music, this raises serious copyright and ownership debates. Can AI borrow from existing works without crossing the line into plagiarism?
- **Deepfakes and Manipulation:** AI can create deepfakes, which are realistic but fake videos and images. While interesting, they raise concerns about misinformation and deception.
- **Bias in Content:** AI models learn from large datasets, which can contain biases. This may lead to biased outputs in text, images, and videos, which can impact hiring algorithms for facial recognition.

6. The Future of Generative AI

Generative AI is moving fast, and the possibilities are **pretty wild**. Here's a peek at what's coming:

- **Fully AI-Created Movies:** Picture an entire film—script, characters, scenes—all made by AI. No director, no camera crew, just pure machine-made creativity.
- **AI-Powered Virtual Worlds:** Future video games and VR may use AI to generate unique landscapes, characters, and storylines for each player's adventure.
- **AI as a Creative Partner:** As AI models become more sophisticated, they could collaborate with artists, musicians, and writers at an even deeper level, co-creating content that neither humans nor machines could produce alone.

MACHINE LEARNING VS. AI: UNDERSTANDING THE DISTINCTIONS

People often use AI (Artificial Intelligence) and ML (Machine Learning) interchangeably, but they're different. Let's break it down.

The Essentials

- **AI:** Think of AI as a high-tech robot that can handle tasks usually done by humans. It can analyze data, recognize patterns, and understand languages—basically, it's the brains behind everything from virtual assistants to self-driving cars.
- **ML:** Machine Learning acts as the robot's brain, enabling AI to learn from data and improve instead of merely following fixed instructions. More data makes it smarter!

The Core Distinction

- **AI** represents the broad concept of creating machines that can think and act intelligently.
- **ML** is the engine that powers AI's most significant capabilities. By absorbing vast amounts of data, ML allows machines to spot patterns, learn from them, and make decisions independently.

Real-World Magic

Machine learning transforms AI from a concept to a practical tool. Rather than following strict rules, ML enables AI to learn from experience and make independent decisions, similar to how practice improves our skills.

Example: Self-Driving Cars

- **AI's Role:** AI is what makes a self-driving car possible. It helps the vehicle recognize roads, traffic signals, and pedestrians to navigate safely.
- **ML's Role:** The car collects data on its proximity to other vehicles, speed, and road conditions. Machine learning processes this information in real-time, continually improving driving decisions.

The Evolution of AI and ML

- **AI's Origins:** Since the mid-20th century, AI aimed to create machines that think and act like humans, a futuristic vision.
- **ML's Impact:** Advances in computing and big data have transformed machine learning from theory to a real-world power source, influencing voice assistants and medical technology.

The Partnership Between AI and ML

- **AI:** Provides the capability to perform complex tasks.
- **ML:** Drives the decision-making process, enabling AI to perform tasks more efficiently and unlock new possibilities.

As AI and ML evolve, their impact on technology, policy, and ethics will continue to grow. These technologies will drive innovation, transform industries, and reshape our lives in powerful and exciting ways.

AI and ML Across Various Fields

These examples illustrate the differences and interplay between AI and machine learning across various industries:

1. Healthcare: AI in Medical Imaging

- **AI:** Systems analyze medical images, such as X-rays, MRIs, or CT scans, to detect anomalies like tumors or diseases.
- **ML:** These systems improve over time by learning from past diagnoses. For example, an ML model can be trained to detect early signs of diabetic retinopathy by studying thousands of previous patient eye scans.

2. Finance: AI in Fraud Detection

- **AI:** Monitors transactions for signs of fraudulent activity.
- **ML:** Analyzes transaction data to distinguish normal behavior from suspicious activity, adapting to new fraud techniques. For

example, ML might recognize that a sudden large transaction in a foreign country, following a pattern of small, local purchases, could be fraudulent.

3. Customer Service: AI Chatbots

- **AI:** Provides 24/7 customer support, answering common questions and assisting with orders.
- **ML:** Improves responses over time by learning from previous interactions, making chatbots more effective and human-like.

4. Retail: AI in Recommendation Systems

- **AI:** E-commerce platforms suggest products based on shopping habits.
- **ML:** Analyzes customer behavior to predict preferences, refining recommendations as it learns from new data.

5. Transportation: AI in Traffic Management

- **AI:** Optimizes city traffic flow by controlling traffic lights and managing congestion.
- **ML:** Predicts traffic patterns by analyzing real-time data and improving traffic management. For example, ML could spot rush-hour bottlenecks and adjust traffic light timings dynamically to improve flow.

6. Entertainment: AI in Content Creation

- **AI:** Creates music, writes articles, or generates visual art.
- **ML:** Learns characteristics of different styles, enabling AI to generate new content that mimics specific artists or genres. For example, an ML model trained in classical compositions might create new pieces that resemble those of Beethoven or Mozart.

7. Manufacturing: AI in Predictive Maintenance

- **AI:** Monitors machines for signs of potential failures, reducing downtime.
- **ML** detects patterns indicating failures. For example, unusual machine vibrations can signal potential part failures, allowing maintenance to be scheduled before costly issues arise.

AI and ML enhance efficiency and responsiveness across industries. Understanding their interplay helps us recognize their impact. AI provides intelligence, while ML ensures continual learning and adaptation. As these technologies evolve, they will unimaginably transform industries and daily life.

DECIPHERING NEURAL NETWORKS

A Beginner's Guide

Neural networks power much of the AI technology we use daily. They enable voice assistants to understand us, assist doctors in diagnosing diseases based on scans, and help self-driving cars navigate!

What makes neural networks unique? Unlike traditional programs that follow strict rules, these networks learn by spotting patterns in large data sets. Instead of being told what to do, they adjust their connections based on observations, improving over time—similar to how we practice and get better.

Convolutional Neural Networks (CNNs)

- CNNs are the go-to AI models for anything image-related. Whether it's spotting handwritten numbers, recognizing faces in photos, or helping self-driving cars avoid obstacles, CNNs are built for the job.
- They use a technique called convolution to analyze small

sections of an image, similar to solving a jigsaw puzzle—each piece reveals part of the whole picture.

Recurrent Neural Networks (RNNs)

RNNs are like built-in AI memory. They're great when the order of information matters—like when trying to predict the next word in a sentence or recognizing speech.

Unlike traditional AI models that process everything simultaneously, RNNs remember past inputs and use that knowledge to make smarter decisions. This makes them a game-changer for speech recognition, language translation, and even writing AI-generated text that flows naturally.

Why RNNs Are Special

- RNNs excel at sequences, making them ideal for tasks where past information influences future decisions, like predictive text and stock market analysis.
- They contain loops that help them remember earlier parts of a sequence—like how you keep track of a storyline while reading a book.
- They're essential for AI systems reliant on context, like chatbots and smart assistants.

How Neural Networks Work

- Imagine a network of **neurons** (represented as dots) connected by lines. These connections allow data to flow through the system.
- Data enters, processes through layers, and exits as results like image identification or sentence translation.
- Each neuron determines how important its input is and adjusts its **weight** accordingly, influencing the final outcome.

How Neural Networks Learn

- RNNs and CNNs learn by trial and error—just like we do when picking up a new skill.
- They tweak their internal settings when they make a mistake (like adjusting a recipe after tasting the first batch).
- This constant feedback loop helps them improve over time, making them more accurate and efficient with every data they process.

Why Neural Networks Matter

- Neural networks power many AI tools daily, including personalized recommendations, voice assistants, and medical diagnosis systems.
- By enabling machines to learn and adapt, neural networks make technology more innovative and valuable in everyday life.

Neural networks are transforming everything from how we interact with devices to advancements in healthcare and transportation. By understanding how these systems learn and remember, we can appreciate their role as game-changers in AI.

Neural networks learn and remember, making them crucial for AI! They enhance interactions with devices and drive progress in healthcare and transportation.

However, as powerful as neural networks are, they raise critical ethical questions. AI systems, including those powered by neural networks, can make decisions that significantly impact people's lives—such as determining who gets a loan, diagnosing medical conditions, or even controlling autonomous vehicles. This power comes with great responsibility.

NLP EXPLAINED: HOW MACHINES UNDERSTAND US

Natural Language Processing (NLP): Bridging the Communication Gap.

Picture this: You're chatting with a friend—cracking jokes, sharing updates, and making weekend plans. Now, imagine having that same kind of effortless back-and-forth with a computer. Sounds wild, right? Well, that's precisely what Natural Language Processing (NLP) is all about—it helps AI understand human language so machines can talk with us in a way that feels natural.

NLP lets computers grasp what we're saying, respond in a way that makes sense, and even hold meaningful conversations. But how does it work? There are a few key pieces that make it all possible. Let's break them down.

Core Components of NLP

1. Syntax

- Syntax dictates how words form grammatically correct sentences. Similarly, NLP enables computers to determine word order and relationships. It analyzes sentence structure, identifies parts of speech, and detects patterns—similar to a grammar checker on steroids.

2. Semantics

- Semantics goes beyond recognizing words; it involves grasping their true meanings. NLP systems analyze individual words and understand the broader context, revealing the intention behind a sentence. This enables AI to discern whether you're asking a question, making a statement, or suggesting something deeper.

3. Pragmatics

Pragmatics examines the context of conversation, focusing on how words are used, not just their meaning. For example, saying, Oh great, another Monday, often implies the opposite of genuine enthusiasm. NLP enables AI to understand nuances like sarcasm and implied meanings instead of interpreting everything literally.

To make sense of human language, NLP uses a few techniques that break down and simplify text, making it easier for machines to process:

- Tokenization splits text into smaller chunks, like individual words or sentences, so that AI can analyze them piece by piece.
- Stemming trims words down to their root form, so running becomes run, making it easier for AI to group similar words.
- Lemmatization, a more advanced version of stemming, ensures that words are reduced to their proper dictionary form—for example, turning better into good.

These techniques simplify the text, making it easier for machines to process and understand.

Real-World Applications of NLP

You probably interact with NLP-powered tools regularly without even realizing it. Here are a few typical applications:

Chatbots: Chatbots are the most common interaction with NLP. Businesses deploy them for customer support or to gather user information. By analyzing your input, they determine your needs and respond effectively—sometimes making it feel like a real conversation.

Speech Recognition Systems: Devices like Alexa and Siri use NLP to understand voice commands. Whether asking for the weather, setting an alarm, or playing a song, they analyze words, grasp context, and respond accordingly.

Sentiment Analysis Tools: Companies track brand opinions using NLP tools that scan social media and reviews, determining if sentiments are positive, negative, or neutral—enhancing understanding of the customer feedback scale.

The Future of NLP: Challenges and Innovations

NLP, or Natural Language Processing, enables computers to understand and communicate with us—but it's imperfect. Language is complex; some words sound alike but have different meanings, and idioms like it's raining cats and dogs are not literal. This complexity poses challenges for AI.

Tools like BERT analyze sentences rather than words, enhancing AI's understanding of meaning and language management.

Machine learning enhances NLP by learning from conversations, adapting to slang, and evolving with language patterns. This improvement makes human-computer interaction smoother across business, education, and healthcare, bridging the gap to technology that once seemed like science fiction.

KNOWLEDGE CHECK: CHAPTER 1

1. What is the difference between Artificial Intelligence (AI) and Machine Learning (ML)?
   A. AI is a type of ML.
   B. ML uses data to train algorithms, while AI covers broader fields like NLP and robotics.
   C. AI is more advanced than ML.
   D. AI is limited to basic tasks, while ML handles complex operations.
2. Which of the following best describes neural networks?
   A. A method for storing data.
   B. A mathematical model that mimics the human brain's neurons to process information.
   C. A tool used exclusively for image recognition.
   D. A hardware system for running AI applications.
3. **True or False:** Natural Language Processing (NLP) enables machines to interpret and generate human language.
4. Short Answer:

What are the two main types of machine learning, and how do they differ?

2

RELIABLE AI RESOURCES FOR BEGINNERS

Exploring AI is like setting out on a big hike—exciting but tricky without the right gear. That's where this chapter comes in! Think of it as your **AI starter pack**, designed to point you to the best tools and learning resources. With so much information out there, it's easy to feel lost, but no worries—I'll help you navigate the essentials so you can **learn efficiently and confidently**.

CURATING YOUR AI LEARNING TOOLKIT: TOP RESOURCES

AI is evolving quickly, and it can be overwhelming to navigate confusing resources. Start with foundational sources that illustrate real-world applications and provide hands-on projects to practice what you learn.

Identifying Comprehensive Resources

Not every AI resource is worth your time. The best ones break things down in a way that makes sense, focus on practical skills, and keep up with AI's rapid changes.

A solid starting point? Websites like Machine Learning Mastery and Towards Data Science.

- They offer beginner-friendly tutorials, case studies, and coding examples.
- Their step-by-step guides make difficult topics easier to understand, so you can see how AI works instead of just reading about it.

What Makes a Great AI Learning Resource?

Not all AI materials are created equal. Some overcomplicate things, while others barely scratch the surface. Here's what to look for when picking the best ones:

- **Credibility**—Select content from reputable experts or institutions. Checking the author's background or site's credibility helps avoid time wasted on unreliable information.
- **Clarity** – The best resources explain AI concepts understandably without oversimplification. You shouldn't need a PhD to understand their basics!
- **Applicability** – AI is hands-on. Choose resources with real-world examples, coding exercises, or projects so you can practice instead of just reading theory.
- **Scalability** –Choose materials that evolve with you, starting with the essentials and progressing to more advanced topics for a smooth transition.

Learn AI in the Way That Works for You

Everyone learns differently. Some people love reading, while others absorb information better through videos, podcasts, or interactive lessons. A mix of formats will help you learn AI faster and retain more:

- **Videos** – Prefer visuals? YouTube channels like CrashCourse

and 3Blue1Brown break down AI topics with animations and step-by-step explanations.
- **Podcasts** – Learning on the go? Try The AI Alignment Podcast or AI in Business for expert insights and discussions on the latest trends.
- **Interactive Tutorials** – Want to get hands-on? Platforms like Kaggle and Codecademy let you experiment with AI and coding in real time.

Mix it up! Experiment with different formats and interactive exercises to find what suits you best. Diverse learning strengthens your AI foundation.

Keeping Your AI Knowledge Fresh

AI moves fast—what was cutting-edge last year might already be outdated. To stay ahead, make sure your learning resources are up to date.

A simple way? Follow AI blogs, news sites, and newsletters that regularly update with breakthroughs, trends, and techniques. Subscribing to AI newsletters delivers fresh insights to your inbox, eliminating the need to search constantly for new material.

By keeping your learning toolkit flexible and filled with high-quality, current resources, you'll always be equipped with the most relevant knowledge. AI isn't standing still, and neither should you. Stay curious, keep learning, and you'll be ready for whatever comes next.

ONLINE PLATFORMS FOR AI LEARNING: WHAT TO CHOOSE AND WHY

Getting started with AI has never been easier. There's no shortage of online platforms offering courses for every skill level—whether you're just dipping your toes in or looking to master advanced techniques. The best part? You can learn at your own pace, from anywhere.

If you're wondering where to start, here are some of the top platforms and what they offer:

- **Coursera** – Partners with top universities and organizations to provide structured courses, guided projects, and peer-supported learning.
- **Udacity** – Known for its nano degree programs, offering hands-on training designed to prepare you for real-world AI jobs.
- **edX** – Founded by Harvard and MIT, covers everything from Python basics to AI-powered data analysis.
- **Fast.ai** – Takes a practical, hands-on approach, making cutting-edge AI techniques accessible to all skill levels.
- DeepLearning.AI – Founded by AI pioneer Andrew Ng, this platform focuses on deep learning and neural networks.

How to Choose the Right AI Learning Platform

Picking the best platform depends on your goals, learning style, and experience level. Here's how to find the right fit:

- **Check the Instructors** – Go for courses taught by experienced professionals or researchers to ensure high-quality content.
- **Prioritize Hands-On Learning** – Engaging projects, fun quizzes, and practical applications help you retain and apply what you learn.
- **Read Reviews** – User feedback on sites like Coursera or Udacity can give you insight into course quality and difficulty level.
- **Free vs. Paid** – Free courses are a great starting point for learning the basics! However, if you're passionate about AI, investing in a paid course can yield valuable certifications, career support, and advanced training to enhance your skills!
- **Choose What Keeps You Engaged** – Choose a platform that

suits how you learn best, whether through structured lessons, interactive exercises, or videos.

Stay Ahead in the Fast-Moving AI Field

AI is evolving fast—what's cutting-edge today might be outdated tomorrow. That's why it's essential to keep learning and stay curious. The best platforms update their courses to keep up with industry trends, so staying engaged with new material will help you stay ahead.

Whether you're looking to boost your career, tackle innovative AI projects, or explore the field out of curiosity, the key is to **stay consistent**. The more you experiment, build, and explore, the more significant impact you'll make in AI.

You can find valuable resources by clicking the link or scanning the QR code to download AI Essentials: Tools, Exercises & Resources.

AI Essentials: Tools, Exercises, and Resources

ESSENTIAL BOOKS AND JOURNALS ON AI FOR BEGINNERS

Exploring AI through books is exciting and enlightening. A well-structured book guides you through AI's complexities, making learning both engaging and manageable.

The right books can transform your understanding. They provide essential ideas and ignite curiosity for deeper exploration. Whether you're starting out or advancing, here are some must-read AI books recommended by the community, especially for beginners!

Core Textbooks

The Hundred-Page Machine Learning Book by **Andriy Burkov**

This beginner-friendly book provides a clear, easy introduction to machine learning. It covers key concepts without overwhelming technical jargon, making it ideal for those seeking a solid foundation in the field.

Machine Learning Yearning by **Andrew Ng**

This book covers structuring machine learning projects effectively. Andrew Ng simplifies complex ideas into practical insights, making it an excellent resource for beginners. It is essential if you want to apply AI to real-world problems with a clear roadmap.

These books provide a solid foundation in AI and machine learning, equipping you to navigate this evolving field. Whether you seek clear concepts or practical insights, these readings will guide you in building real AI knowledge step by step.

To download the free book, click on the link or scan the QR code:

Machine Learning Yearning.

Hands-On Machine Learning with Scikit-Learn, Keras, and TensorFlow by **Aurélien Géron**

This book is perfect for those seeking practical experience. It guides readers through tools like Scikit-Learn and TensorFlow, applying machine learning concepts to real-world scenarios.

These textbooks are ideal for self-study. They feature clear examples, illustrations, and case studies that can be meaningfully applied.

Accessible Authors

Some authors have a unique ability to make complex subjects approachable. A few standout names include:

The Master Algorithm by **Pedro Domingos**

This book examines the search for a unifying algorithm for all machine-learning approaches. Domingos details five major schools of machine learning, discussing their strengths and limitations engagingly. Whether you're a beginner or curious about AI's future, The Master Algorithm offers insights into machine learning and potential advancements in AI.

Artificial Intelligence: A Modern Approach by **Stuart Russell and Peter Norvig**

This widely used textbook provides a comprehensive introduction to AI, presenting material that is accessible for newcomers yet valuable for experienced readers readers.

Journals and Periodicals

To stay informed about AI research and trends, consider reading:

- AI Magazine
- Journal of Artificial Intelligence Research (JAIR)

These publications provide accessible summaries of key AI research and trends, helping readers stay connected to the latest developments in the field.

Reading Strategies for AI Books and Journals

AI books and journals can be dense. To avoid feeling overwhelmed:

- tart with summaries or executive summaries to grasp key points.
- Focus on specific chapters or articles that align with your learning goals.
- Use note-taking or mind-mapping techniques to retain and organize key concepts.

Use these strategies to navigate AI literature and reinforce learning gradually.

FOLLOWING THE RIGHT EXPERTS: BLOGS AND SOCIAL MEDIA TO WATCH

In the fast-paced AI world, keeping up with trends and breakthroughs can feel like drinking from a firehose—there's so much happening!

Following key AI influencers helps you stay updated on significant developments and diverse perspectives shaping AI's future. Whether a beginner or deeply involved, the right experts can greatly enhance your learning and growth in AI.

Influential AI Thinkers

Identifying which influencers to follow can significantly enhance your understanding and keep you informed about the state of AI.

- **Sebastian Thrun,** founder of Udacity and co-founder of Google X, has significantly impacted AI, especially in autonomous driving and online education. He discusses AI's influence on technology, education, and future work.

- **Yann LeCun**, Meta's Chief AI Scientist, is a deep learning pioneer known for his work in convolutional neural networks (CNNs). He often shares insights on AI ethics and policy.

Following these experts gives you access to cutting-edge AI knowledge and fresh perspectives on AI and its future implications.

Blog Resources

- **Andrej Karpathy,** former Director of AI at Tesla, writes about deep learning, AI research, and software engineering on his blog. His clear and in-depth explanations make it a valuable resource for AI enthusiasts and professionals.
- **The Gradient** – A research-driven blog covering AI breakthroughs, ethical discussions, and interviews with industry leaders. It's an excellent resource for staying informed about the latest AI trends.
- **Google AI Blog** – Google's AI research blog provides insights into state-of-the-art AI innovations, research papers, and industry applications.

Social Media Influencers

Platforms like Twitter and LinkedIn can be powerful learning tools, as many AI professionals and educators share their insights, research findings, and opinions.

- **Fei-Fei Li**, co-director of the Stanford Human-Centered AI Institute, frequently discusses AI's societal impact, ethics, and inclusivity. Her Twitter and LinkedIn posts highlight the importance of responsible AI development.
- **Andrew Ng,** founder of DeepLearning.AI and co-founder of Coursera, shares AI education, research advancements, and career advice on LinkedIn and Twitter. His content is ideal for professionals looking to deepen their AI knowledge.

Podcasts and Interviews

Listening to AI experts is another effective way to stay informed:

- **Lex Fridman Podcast** – Features long-form discussions with AI pioneers, researchers, and industry leaders, offering deep insights into AI, machine learning, and broader technological trends.
- **AI Today Podcast** – A beginner-friendly podcast that simplifies AI concepts and features interviews with AI experts discussing real-world applications.
- **The TWIML AI Podcast** – Hosted by Sam Charrington- explores cutting-edge AI research and industry trends through expert interviews.

LEVERAGING UNIVERSITY AND ONLINE COURSE RESOURCES

Getting into AI doesn't mean you must shell out big bucks or sit in a lecture hall. Thanks to top universities, world-class AI education is just a few clicks away! Institutions like MIT and Stanford offer free open courseware, so anyone with an internet connection can dive into AI without spending a dime.

What's even more incredible? These courses often mirror what's taught on campus, giving you access to the same high-quality materials that students at these prestigious schools use. Whether you're just starting or looking to sharpen your skills, these free resources are an incredible way to learn AI on your own terms.

Here's how you can make the most of these resources:

- **MIT's OpenCourseWare (OCW)** offers **free** AI and machine learning courses, including lecture notes, assignments, exams, and video lectures from past MIT classes. While it provides

valuable learning resources, it does not offer certificates or direct interaction with instructors.
    - **Example Course:** *Introduction to Deep Learning* (MIT 6.S191)
- **Stanford Online** provides free and paid AI-related courses, including deep learning, machine learning, and natural language processing. Courses range from introductory to advanced levels and are taught by Stanford professors. Some courses offer certificates through platforms like Coursera and edX.
    - **Example Course:** *Machine Learning by Andrew Ng* (available on Coursera)

Both platforms allow you to learn at your own pace, giving you the flexibility to explore AI topics that match your interests and fit your schedule. This is especially valuable if you balance work, school, or other commitments while developing your AI skills.

Formal education isn't the only way to master AI. The best approach combines structured courses with informal tools, such as blogs, podcasts, and projects- for a rewarding learning experience that merges theory and practice.

- **Hands-on Projects** – Explore real-world AI projects on GitHub, where you can analyze open-source code and contribute.
- **Problem-Solving Challenges** – Platforms like HackerRank, Kaggle, and LeetCode let you apply your skills to coding challenges and machine-learning competitions, reinforcing what you've learned.

When selecting courses, consider your current knowledge level and long-term goals. Here's a guide to help you decide:

- **Beginners**: Start with introductory AI, Python, or data science courses to build a strong foundation. Courses like Andrew Ng's Machine Learning on Coursera are great entry points.

- **Intermediate Learners** – Focus on machine learning frameworks like TensorFlow and PyTorch and projects that apply AI to real-world problems.
- **Advanced Learners** – Dive into specialized topics such as neural networks, deep learning, natural language processing (NLP), and even quantum computing to deepen your expertise.

Benefits of Structured Learning

- **Systematic Learning** – Courses guide you step by step, ensuring you understand the basics before tackling advanced material.
- **Peer Interaction & Mentorship** – Many online platforms provide forums, study groups, or direct instructor interactions, which help clarify complex concepts.
- **Community & Motivation** – Learning with others keeps you engaged, accountable, and inspired, making it easier to stay on track.

Combining formal courses with hands-on practice and AI communities creates a well-rounded learning ecosystem that helps you understand, apply, and innovate with AI. AI is an evolving field, and your learning journey will be as dynamic as the technology. From structured courses to self-guided projects, you can shape your education to fit your goals and interests.

This chapter introduced you to essential resources and strategies for learning AI. As you explore further, you'll be ready to tackle advanced, innovative aspects of AI—unlocking opportunities for creativity, problem-solving, and career growth.

KNOWLEDGE CHECK: CHAPTER 2

1. Which platform is known for offering free online AI courses?
   A. Udemy
   B. Coursera
   C. IBM SkillsBuild
   D. LinkedIn Learning

2. Which of the following should NOT be used as a reliable source for Learning AI?
   A. AI-powered vacuum cleaners
   B. Scientific journals
   C. AI-specific blogs by leading experts
   D. Random videos on social media without any citations
   E. Online AI courses offered by universities

3. **True or False:** Following AI experts on social media can help you stay current on trends and breakthroughs.

4. Short Answer:
   A. Name two online platforms that provide free or affordable AI learning resources for beginners.

3

THE SUBTLE INTELLIGENCE POWERING YOUR WORLD

Imagine entering after a long day. The lights adjust to your favorite setting, creating a warm atmosphere. Your AI assistant suggests a recipe based on fridge ingredients, sparing you the What's for dinner? dilemma. While cooking, your assistant plays your favorite playlist, relaxing everything.

This is not just about convenience—it's a glimpse into a future where AI anticipates your needs, personalizes experiences, and elevates your life.

Whether you love tech or are new to smart home technology, integrating AI makes your space more responsive, efficient, and secure. It redefines what it means to feel comfortable at home.

SMART HOME DEVICES: ENHANCING YOUR LIVING SPACE WITH AI

AI technology has made homes smarter, enhancing daily life in practical ways:

- **Smart Thermostats:** Devices like Google Nest and Ecobee use AI to learn your habits and adjust heating and cooling automatically for optimal energy use comfort.
- **Smart Lighting Systems:** Philips Hue and LIFX let you control lighting remotely, set schedules, adjust brightness, and change colors based on time or mood. Some integrate with motion sensors and AI assistants automation.
- **AI-Powered Security Systems:** Devices like Ring, Arlo, and Google Nest Cam utilize motion detection, facial recognition, and adaptive learning to send real-time alerts for unusual activities and recognize familiar faces, adjusting security routines accordingly.

These devices aren't just gadgets—they learn your preferences and automate daily routines to make life easier and more intuitive.

Benefits of Smart Home AI Integration

- **Save Energy:** Smart thermostats (Nest, Ecobee) and AI lighting (Philips Hue, LIFX) adjust automatically based on occupancy and schedules, cutting energy use and lowering bills.
- **Convenience:** I-driven automation allows remote control of your home's features through apps, voice assistants, or predictive settings that adjust automatically.
- **Enhanced Security:** AI cameras and alarms (e.g., Ring, Arlo, Nest Cam) enhance security by detecting motion, recognizing faces, and sending real-time threat alerts. Some integrate with emergency services for added support protection.

Setting Up a Smart Home

- **Start Simple:** Use a hub like Google Nest or Amazon Alexa to manage multiple devices from one place.
- **Choose Compatible Devices:** Select smart lights, thermostats, or security systems that fit your needs.

- **Easy Setup:** Connect devices to Wi-Fi and follow app instructions for quick installation.

Popular Smart Home Hubs

- **Amazon Echo (with Alexa)** – Voice-controlled hub that integrates with thousands of smart home devices.
- **Google Nest Hub** – Google Assistant-powered smart display that controls connected home devices.
- **Apple HomePod (with Siri)** – Works as a HomeKit hub, enabling secure smart home automation.
- **Samsung SmartThings Hub** – One of the most versatile smart home hubs, supporting Zigbee, Z-Wave, and Wi-Fi devices.
- **Aeotec Smart Home Hub** – The official replacement for the discontinued SmartThings Hub, compatible with SmartThings software.
- **Hubitat Elevation** – A powerful local automation hub that doesn't rely on the cloud.
- **Homey Pro** – A premium multi-protocol smart home hub supporting Z-Wave, Zigbee, Wi-Fi, and Bluetooth.
- **Amazon Echo Hub** – A newer wall-mounted smart home control center (introduced in 2023).
- **Aqara Hub M2** – A strong choice for HomeKit users, supporting Zigbee and IR remote control.

Real-Life Examples

- **Personal Fitness**: A busy executive used the AI-powered fitness app Future, which provided personalized workout plans and real-time feedback. Over six months, they improved their health without needing a personal trainer.
- **Mental Health**: A college student with anxiety used Wysa, an AI mental health app. It offered stress-relief exercises, CBT techniques, and mood tracking. Interacting with Wysa's

chatbot helped the student feel calmer and more in control emotions.
- **Energy Efficiency**: A family installed the Google Nest Learning Thermostat to reduce energy costs. The AI adjusted the home's temperature based on their habits, leading to a 15% savings on their energy bills.
- **Elderly Care**: An older woman used CarePredict, a wearable AI device that tracked her daily activities. The device alerted her family to any irregular patterns, allowing her to live independently while staying safe.
- **Personalized Education**: A middle school student struggling with math used DreamBox, an AI learning platform that adapted lessons to their unique learning style. This helped the student gain confidence and improve their grades.

AI is transforming everyday life, making homes smarter, routines simpler, and security stronger. Whether in fitness, learning, or caregiving, AI provides personalized, responsive solutions that enhance our quality of life and unlock new possibilities.

PERSONAL FINANCE AND AI: BUDGETING AND INVESTMENT TOOLS

Managing money can sometimes feel overwhelming, but AI is here to make it simpler and smarter. Whether it's budgeting, investing, or tracking expenses, AI tools are effortlessly helping people take control of their finances. Here's how:

AI in Budgeting

Budgeting is key to managing finances, but it can be tedious. AI budgeting tools like PocketGuard simplify the process by:

- Analyzing your spending habits
- Categorizing transactions
- Offering personalized recommendations

AI in Investments

Investing once meant paying high fees to a financial advisor, but AI has changed that game. Tools like Betterment and Wealthfront use artificial intelligence to help make wise investment decisions on your behalf. Here's how it works:

- You set your goals (like saving for college or retirement) and your comfort level with risk.
- The AI takes over, analyzing market trends and adjusting your investments for the best returns.
- This makes investing easy for everyone, regardless of experience. AI works fast, allowing it to react quickly to market changes to protect your money.

Security Considerations

Using AI for money management is helpful, but keeping your data secure is essential. Reputable AI apps protect your information with:

- **Encryption:** Scrambling your data so it's unreadable to hackers.
- **Two-Factor Authentication:** Requiring a code sent to your phone or email to log in.
- **Secure Servers:** Storing your data safely.

Use trusted apps with clear privacy policies to ensure your info is safe. Regularly update your software and use strong, unique passwords to secure your accounts. These simple steps significantly enhance your security.

Future of AI in Personal Finance

AI is only getting smarter. In the future, it might:

- Predict significant life changes, like buying a house or having a baby, and help you plan ahead.

- Work with smart devices in your home, factoring in expenses such as car maintenance and energy usage to refine your budget.

These advancements could make managing your money even easier and more personalized to your life.

AI is transforming money management, simplifying budgeting and investing for everyone. These tools save time and enable smarter financial decisions, allowing you to focus on what matters.

AI-POWERED APPS TO KEEP YOU HEALTHY

Living a Healthy Lifestyle with AI

Living a healthy lifestyle can sometimes feel like a lot to keep up with, but AI-powered apps are making it easier to manage your wellness. These tools track your health, create personalized fitness and nutrition plans, and support your mental well-being. Let's look at how AI is changing the game regarding staying healthy.

Health Monitoring with AI

AI acts like a personal health assistant, using your phone or wearable devices to track vital signs such as:

- **Heart Rate:** Smartwatches monitor your heart and alert you to irregularities.
- **Sleep:** Apps analyze phases like REM and deep sleep, offering tips for improving rest.
- **Activity:** Fitness trackers count your steps, measure calories burned, and even remind you to move.

These metrics are often combined into a health dashboard on your phone, giving you a complete view of your well-being.

Personalized Fitness and Nutrition

AI apps tailor workout and meal plans to your goals and preferences:

- **Fitness:** Apps create exercise routines based on your fitness level and adjust them as you progress.
- **Nutrition:** Meal-planning apps suggest recipes that match your dietary needs and allergies, updating based on your feedback.

This customization ensures that your fitness and diet plans evolve with you, making it easier to stick to your health goals.

AI for Mental Health

AI is also helping people manage their mental well-being:

- **Chatbots:** Tools like Woebot use therapy techniques to guide users through managing anxiety and stress.
- **Mood Tracking:** Apps analyze your mood entries to identify patterns and suggest helpful actions.
- **Accessible Therapy:** AI chatbots provide a private, judgment-free space to discuss feelings and receive support.

These tools make mental health care more accessible, especially for those hesitant to seek traditional therapy.

Protecting Your Health Data

Since these apps handle sensitive personal information, security is essential. To keep your data safe:

- Choose apps from trusted developers with clear privacy policies.
- Look for compliance with regulations like HIPAA in the U.S.
- Regularly update apps and carefully review permissions.

Taking these steps ensures you can enjoy the benefits of AI health tools while keeping your information secure.

A Healthier Future with AI

AI transforms health and fitness with personalized, data-driven insights that simplify staying healthy. From tracking sleep to promoting activity and supporting mental well-being, these tools help you achieve your health goals. As AI advances, it discovers more ways to enhance our lives.

ENTERTAINMENT AND AI: HOW ALGORITHMS INFLUENCE WHAT YOU WATCH AND LISTEN TO

AI impacts entertainment, influencing how we watch movies, listen to music, and choose books. Streaming services like Netflix and Spotify utilize AI to recommend content based on user habits. When you binge on sci-fi or listen to jazz, AI learns your preferences and suggests similar content. These algorithms analyze behavior for personalized recommendations.

AI in Streaming Services

Artificial intelligence quietly plays the roles of director, curator, and game developer, all rolled into one:

- **Netflix and Hulu:** Analyze your watch history, ratings, and time spent on shows to suggest what you'll enjoy next.
- **Spotify and Apple Music:** Recommend playlists and songs by learning your listening habits.

These systems adapt over time, becoming smarter the more you use them. Thus, your entertainment experience becomes seamless and personalized.

AI in Gaming

AI also transforms gaming by making it more immersive and adaptive:

- **Responsive NPCs:** AI manages NPCs that react to your choices, enhancing gameplay realism.
- **Adjustable Difficulty:** AI tailors challenges to your skill level, ensuring the game remains engaging without becoming frustrating.

This customization allows players to enhance their experience with games suited to their pace and style.

AI in Book Recommendations

Online bookstores like Amazon use AI to suggest books based on:

- Your browsing history
- Past purchases
- Time spent reading specific genres.

These recommendations introduce readers to new authors and genres, enhancing the reading experience.

Ethical Concerns in AI Entertainment

While AI improves entertainment, it raises ethical issues:

- **Bias in Recommendations:** If trained on narrow data, AI might favor specific genres or demographics, limiting exposure to diverse content.
- **Privacy Concerns:** Collecting personal data, such as viewing or listening habits, must be handled securely and transparently.

Platforms must address these challenges to ensure fair, unbiased recommendations and protect user data.

The Future of AI in Entertainment

AI has transformed entertainment, making it more interactive and personalized. Smarter recommendations and immersive games enhance our leisure time. As technology evolves, the lines between creators, content, and consumers blur, promising even more innovation experiences!

AI IN PERSONAL ORGANIZATION AND PRODUCTIVITY TOOLS

Managing time and tasks can be overwhelming, but AI tools enhance efficiency. From scheduling meetings to tracking emails, AI streamlines your routine and keeps you organized.

AI-Driven Scheduling Tools

Setting up meetings used to mean juggling calendars and endless emails. Now, AI tools like Calendly and x.ai automate the process:

- They scan everyone's schedules to suggest the best times.
- They send invitations and reminders automatically.

These tools save time and eliminate the hassle, letting you focus on more critical tasks.

Email Management and AI

Dealing with a cluttered inbox can be exhausting. AI-powered email tools like Superhuman and features in Gmail help by:

- Prioritizing important emails based on your habits.
- Suggesting quick replies.
- Unsubscribing you from unwanted newsletters.

These tools learn from how you use your email, so they get better at helping you manage your inbox over time.

AI in Task Management

AI takes task management to the next level by:

- Predicting how long tasks will take.

- Automatically setting deadlines.
- Prioritizing tasks based on urgency and your work habits.

Tools like Asana and Trello enhance productivity by utilizing AI to automate workflows, predict timelines, and manage tasks effectively. Asana evaluates workloads, recommends deadlines, and automates repetitive tasks, while Trello's Butler tool optimizes routines with rule-based triggers. By minimizing manual work, these tools ensure projects stay on track and allow more time for critical tasks.

Long-Term Benefits

AI doesn't just help with day-to-day tasks—it improves your overall productivity and well-being:

- **Time Savings:** By automating routine work, you have more creative and personal growth time.
- **Reduced Stress:** With AI managing your schedule, you can stay on track without feeling overwhelmed.
- **Better Balance:** Smart automation makes it easier to achieve a healthier work-life balance.

A Smarter Way to Stay Organized

AI-powered productivity tools are transforming how we manage our time and tasks. They help you complete more on your to-do list and make work more fulfilling and enjoyable. As these technologies improve, they'll better align with your needs, allowing you to focus on what truly matters counts.

KNOWLEDGE CHECK: CHAPTER 3

1. Which of these AI applications is commonly used in smart homes?
    A. Face recognition software
    B. Virtual personal assistants like Alexa or Google Home
    C. Machine learning models
    D. Self-driving cars

2. Which AI-powered tool is widely used to help with personal finance?
    A. AI-powered vacuum cleaners
    B. Chatbots
    C. AI-based budgeting apps
    D. AI-driven virtual reality games
3. **True or False:** AI can help personalize your entertainment options, such as music and streaming recommendations.
4. Short Answer:

Name one way AI is commonly used in healthcare to improve daily life.

4

UTILIZING AI IN YOUR CAREER

AI is shaking up the marketing world in ways we never thought possible. It's no longer just about catchy slogans and flashy ads—it's about understanding people on a whole new level. AI helps businesses track trends, predict what customers want, and personalize every interaction. That's why those online ads seem to read your mind. AI analyzes your clicks, searches, and habits to put the right content in front of you at the perfect moment.

HOW AI IS SHAKING UP MARKETING

This isn't just a cool business feature—it's a game-changer. AI can take the guesswork out of marketing by showing what works, what flops, and what needs tweaking. Whether you're running a startup, managing a brand, or just trying to stay ahead in your field, knowing how AI plays into marketing gives you an edge. Let's get into how it works and how you can use it to your advantage.

Leveraging AI for Targeted Marketing Campaigns

Let's say you're running a clothing brand and want to launch a new line of eco-friendly shoes. Your audience is pretty broad, but who's really going to love these new kicks? That's where AI comes in handy.

AI tools like Google Analytics and HubSpot can dig through tons of data from your website, social media, and even customer emails to figure out who's most likely to buy. You might find out that eco-conscious millennials who have already bought your eco-bags are your perfect target audience. With this info, you can whip up a marketing campaign just for them—showing off ads that highlight how your new shoes are made from recycled materials or giving them a special discount.

By doing this, AI helps you skip the spray-and-pray marketing method—where you send the same message to everyone and hope for the best. Instead, AI makes sure you're talking directly to people who care about what you're offering, which leads to better engagement and more sales.

Chatbots: Your 24/7 Customer Support Buddy

Chatbots are changing the game in customer service by offering help around the clock, any day of the week. These AI-powered bots can tackle a variety of customer questions without needing a human to step in, whether it's answering common queries or helping with orders and bookings. What's cool is that they learn from every interaction, getting better over time, which makes them super useful. This ability to learn means they can handle more complicated questions more efficiently, ensuring a fast, reliable, and scalable service.

Picture this: a customer is browsing your online store late at night, trying to find info about a product. An AI chatbot can jump in right away, answer their questions, and even suggest other products they might like. This not only makes the shopping experience better but also boosts the chances of making a sale. Plus, chatbots take the load off your human customer service team, allowing them to focus on trickier issues, which ultimately enhances overall efficiency and keeps customers happy.

AI-Driven Content Creation

Creating great content is essential for successful marketing, but it requires time and resources. AI helps automate content creation, from social media to news articles. Natural language generation (NLG) software analyzes data to produce informative, well-structured, human-like content. This saves time and maintains a strong online presence, crucial for connecting with customers and enhancing brand visibility.

For example, an AI tool can track industry trends and generate numerous blog posts that position your company as a thought leader. These posts can align with your brand's voice and be optimized for search engines, increasing online visibility and driving site traffic. This enhances your content strategy and allows your creative team to focus on more strategic projects, utilizing their skills effectively.

Measuring Campaign Effectiveness

One of the coolest things about AI in marketing is how it helps you measure and analyze how well your campaigns are doing. AI tools can keep tabs on all sorts of metrics, like click-through rates, engagement levels, and even sales conversions. When you use these tools in your marketing efforts, you get real-time insights into what's working and what's not. This quick feedback lets you tweak your campaigns on the fly, making them more effective and boosting your ROI.

Plus, AI-driven analytics can dig deeper into customer behavior and preferences, which helps you fine-tune your marketing strategies over time. For example, by figuring out which types of content get the most engagement or which marketing channels work best, you can use your resources more wisely and focus on the strategies that really pay off.

Bringing AI into your marketing game can totally change how you connect with customers, create content, and measure your campaign success. As you start using these AI tools and strategies, you'll not only amp up your marketing efforts but also drive some serious business growth, keeping your brand competitive in today's fast-paced digital world. As you keep exploring AI applications in different professional areas, you'll find even more ways to weave this powerful tech into your career, boosting your skills and opening up fresh opportunities for innovation and growth.

AI FOR PROJECT MANAGERS: ENHANCING DECISION-MAKING AND EFFICIENCY

Managing Projects with AI: Work Smarter, Not Harder

Managing projects can be a bit like juggling, right? You've got to keep an eye on tasks, work with your team, stay within budget, and hit those deadlines. Luckily, AI is around to help you keep everything on track and make sure you don't miss a beat with any of these crucial tasks.

Smarter Project Scheduling

Imagine you're juggling a construction project with a tight deadline, where different teams are tackling various tasks, and then bam—unexpected delays hit, like bad weather messing with your plans. AI tools like Trello and Monday.com can really help you stay on top of these challenges and keep everything moving forward.

For example, if AI looks at past construction projects and sees that roofing takes longer when it rains, it might suggest tweaking your schedule or adding some extra time to avoid those pesky delays. This makes planning a lot smoother and helps you dodge any last-minute surprises.

A great example is Procore, a construction management platform that uses AI to help project managers keep track of timelines, costs, and risks. It even throws out suggestions to optimize workflows, making sure everything runs like a well-oiled machine.

Proactive Risk Management

AI is great at spotting problems before they turn into big headaches. Imagine you're working on a software project—tools like RiskIQ can keep an eye on things and let you know if something's going off track. Maybe one team is lagging behind, or there's a holdup in getting a crucial piece of software approved. Instead of rushing to fix things at the last minute, AI helps you step in early and tweak your plan ahead of time.

In real life, the Rio Tinto mining company uses AI to predict equipment failures before they happen, which helps avoid expensive delays. In project management, having this kind of insight can save you time, money, and a lot of stress.

Enhancing Team Collaboration

AI is really changing the game when it comes to teamwork! Tools like Slack and Microsoft Teams are using AI to make communication smoother and more efficient. They automatically organize discussions, set reminders, and even suggest the best times for team meetings based on everyone's availability. It's like having a personal assistant that helps keep everyone on the same page!

Take Asana, for example. It's packed with AI features that can actually notice when certain team members are swamped with too many tasks. When that happens, it suggests redistributing the workload to ensure that no one feels overwhelmed. This way, the project stays on track, and everyone can contribute without feeling stressed out. It's all about making collaboration easier and more enjoyable for everyone involved.

Real-Time Data for Faster Decisions

As a project manager, you're always in the thick of decision-making—whether it's about shifting resources around, tweaking timelines, or adjusting budgets. The cool thing is that AI tools are here to lend a hand by providing real-time data, which means you can make quicker and smarter choices.

Let's say you're in charge of a marketing campaign, and you spot an ad that's just not hitting the mark. Instead of sticking with it, AI can step in and suggest that you move some of that budget to ads that are actually getting people's attention. This kind of instant feedback is super helpful because it lets you make changes on the fly, keeping your project running smoothly and effectively. So, with AI by your side, you can stay agile and responsive, making sure your projects are not just on track but also thriving.

The Future of AI in Project Management

Incorporating AI into your career—whether you're in marketing, project management, or any other field—feels like adding a superpower to your toolkit. Seriously, it's like having a secret weapon! AI helps you work smarter instead of harder, taking care of the heavy lifting when it comes to data analysis, scheduling tasks, and even predicting potential problems before they arise. As AI keeps getting better and more advanced, those who jump on the bandwagon will definitely have the upper hand. Embracing this technology means you can bring fresh ideas and greater efficiency to everything you do at work. So, why not leverage this amazing tool to elevate your career and stay ahead of the game?

THE ROLE OF AI IN DATA-DRIVEN DECISION MAKING

Predictive analytics is all about using artificial intelligence to dig into past data and make educated guesses about future trends. It's like having a crystal ball for decision-making! Retailers really love this tool because it helps them figure out what products will be in demand, which in turn makes managing their inventory a whole lot easier and boosts their profits.

In the finance world, predictive analytics is a game-changer too. It helps investors get a sense of how stocks might perform, which can be super helpful when deciding where to put their money. At the end of the day, predictive analytics takes all that historical data and turns it into insights that you can actually act on. This means businesses can make smarter, data-driven decisions that not only reduce risks but also sharpen their strategic planning. So, whether you're in retail or finance, embracing predictive analytics can really give you an edge.

AI in Business Intelligence

AI is really stepping up the game in the world of business intelligence (BI). When you mix AI with BI tools, it's like giving businesses a superpower to enhance their analysis, visualize tricky data trends, and discover insights that are often hard to spot. AI algorithms are like data detectives, efficiently sifting through massive datasets to find patterns that can shape smart business strategies.

For example, AI can dive into consumer behavior to uncover purchasing trends, which helps companies fine-tune their marketing strategies. Plus, AI-powered BI tools make data visualization a breeze. They present information in a way that's super easy to understand, even for folks who might not have a background in data analysis. These visualizations are a game-changer, allowing stakeholders to quickly grasp important insights and make well-informed decisions without getting lost in the numbers. Overall, the integration of AI into BI is transforming how businesses operate, making them more agile and insightful than ever before.

Case Studies of Successful Implementations

AI in Retail – Walmart's Inventory Management

One of the coolest examples of AI in action is Walmart, the huge retail powerhouse we all know. Every day, Walmart deals with a staggering amount of customer data. To keep shelves stocked with popular items, retailers use AI to predict hot sellers.

By looking at sales trends, weather changes, and even local happenings, Walmart's AI system can predict what items shoppers are likely to want in the upcoming weeks. For instance, if a holiday or a big sporting event is just around the corner, the system gets smart and expects a spike in demand for things like barbecue grills and snacks. This way, customers can always find what they're looking for, and

Walmart can boost its profits by steering clear of both overstocking and understocking. It's a win-win situation.

AI in Healthcare – Mayo Clinic's Diagnosis Support System

The Mayo Clinic is really stepping up its game by using AI to enhance how patients are diagnosed and treated. They've rolled out an AI system that assists doctors in sifting through patient symptoms and medical histories, helping them come up with possible diagnoses and treatment options.

For example, when a patient walks in with chest pain, this AI system can quickly pull up information from thousands of similar cases and relevant medical studies. It can suggest potential diagnoses like heart disease or acid reflux, which is pretty impressive! This capability allows doctors to make quicker and more accurate decisions, which could potentially save lives. Plus, the cool part is that the system keeps learning from new data, so it just gets better and better over time, leading to even higher-quality care for patients.

These case studies really highlight how transformative AI can be in decision-making across different industries. By harnessing the power of AI to analyze data and generate insights, organizations can make smarter, more strategic decisions that fuel success and spark innovation. As AI technology keeps advancing, its role in decision-making is only going to grow, opening up exciting new opportunities for growth and progress in a wide range of professional fields.

The Challenges of AI in Decision-Making

Using AI for decision-making definitely has its perks, but it also comes with a few bumps in the road. One major thing to keep in mind is that the quality of insights generated by AI really hinges on how accurate and reliable the input data is. This means that managing data properly is super important.

Take Facebook, for instance. They use AI to recommend content and ads tailored to what users like based on their data. But if the data management isn't up to par, it can lead to misinformation spreading like wildfire across the platform. This really underscores the importance of having solid controls in place to prevent such issues.

Then there's the whole privacy aspect to consider. AI systems often need to work with huge amounts of data, which raises some serious ethical questions about how that data is used and who gets access to it. In the healthcare sector, for example, it's crucial that patient data stays secure. AI systems in this field have to follow strict privacy laws, like HIPAA, to ensure that sensitive information is protected. So, while AI can be a powerful tool, it's essential to navigate these challenges carefully to make the most of its potential.

The Future of AI in Decision-Making

AI will become smarter, helping us make decisions. With more data and evolving technology, expect advanced systems that analyze information quickly and accurately. From personalizing school learning to predicting climate change, AI is set to significantly influence our future future.

Let's be real—AI in decision-making isn't just a fad; it's the way of the future. By tapping into the power of data, AI gives individuals and organizations the tools to make smarter, more informed choices that will influence our world for many years ahead. From spotting the next big trend in fashion to enhancing healthcare outcomes, AI is truly transforming how we make decisions and helping us navigate an increasingly complicated world. It's an exciting time to see how this technology will continue to evolve and impact our lives.

ENHANCING CUSTOMER SERVICE WITH AI TECHNOLOGIES

Customer service is super important for any business that wants to succeed. It's basically the bridge between a company and its customers, where trust gets built, problems get sorted out, and solid relationships are created. But here's the thing: as businesses expand

and the world gets more interconnected, dealing with customer questions and issues around the clock can be quite a challenge.

That's where Artificial Intelligence (AI) comes in! AI is revolutionizing customer service, making it faster, smarter, and more efficient. Let's take a closer look at how AI is transforming customer support—it's an exciting shift for everyone involved.

AI Chatbots: Your Friendly, 24/7 Support

AI chatbots have changed the way we handle customer service. They're available 24/7, so you can reach out for help whenever needed—no waiting around like you would with human agents! For example, if you're shopping online and want to check on your order status late at night, you can chat with a bot. It's super convenient because you'll get instant updates instead of waiting for an email response or until the next business day. It's like having a helpful assistant at your fingertips, ready to provide answers whenever needed.

These chatbots do more than track orders. They can:

- Answer product-related questions
- Resolve basic technical issues.
- Identify patterns in customer reports to suggest solutions.
- Escalate complex problems to human experts when necessary.

By automating routine queries, AI chatbots enhance efficiency and allow human agents to focus on more complex customer needs.

Learning and Getting Smarter

One of the coolest things about AI is how it learns and improves over time. The more it chats with people, the sharper it becomes at answering questions and solving issues. This whole process is called machine learning, and it means AI is always on the up and up, improving itself continuously.

Take, for instance, an AI fashion chatbot. It's like having a personal shopping buddy who helps you find clothes you'll love based on what you like. With every conversation, this chatbot gets better at suggesting outfits, almost like it's picking up on your unique style.

What's really neat is that AI doesn't just spit out the same old generic answers. Instead, it becomes more precise and useful as it collects more information. So, the more you engage with AI, the more it tunes into your needs and preferences, making your experience smoother and more enjoyable. It's like having a helper that's always learning how to serve you better.

Personalizing Your Experience

AI is making customer service more personal than ever. By analyzing data like shopping history and browsing habits, AI can offer tailored recommendations, special deals, and customized experiences that feel relevant to each customer.

Take Spotify, for example. Its AI tracks what you listen to and curates playlists based on your taste, making music discovery feel effortless. Similarly, Amazon suggests products based on past purchases and browsing behavior, helping customers find what they need without searching endlessly.

This level of personalization makes customers feel understood while also benefiting businesses by strengthening relationships and increasing engagement. As AI continues to improve, we can expect even more intuitive and seamless experiences that make shopping, streaming, and interacting with brands more convenient and enjoyable.

Voice Recognition: Talking to AI Like It's a Human

Hey there! So, you've probably seen how much better recognition tech has gotten lately, right? Virtual assistants like Siri from Apple, Alexa from Amazon, and Google Assistant are pretty impressive—they can actually understand what you say and respond almost like they're chatting with you in person. But it's not just about playing your favorite tunes or giving you the weather update; voice recognition is stepping up the game in customer service, too.

In call centers, these AI-powered voice systems are super handy. They can route your call to the right department, handle simple tasks like password resets, or even assist human agents while they're on the line with you. So, when you're talking to a customer service rep, AI can quickly pull up the info they need and help them give you faster and more accurate answers.

For instance, if you call your bank because you've lost your credit card, an AI system might instantly recognize your issue and connect you straight to the right department. This way, you skip all the annoying menu options and get the help you need without any hassle. It's all about making things smoother and more efficient for everyone involved.

Improving Customer Service Through Feedback Analysis

AI isn't just a handy tool for chatting with customers; it's also a game-changer for businesses looking to up their service game by digging into customer feedback. Whenever someone drops a review, shoots off an email, or shares a thought on social media, it's like gold for the company—it reveals how they're really doing.

AI can comb through all this info, spot trends, and point out where the business could step up its game. For example, imagine a restaurant chain that's getting a ton of online reviews complaining about long wait times. With AI on the case, those reviews can be analyzed, and the issue can be flagged for the management team. This way, the restaurant can zero in on fixing those wait times and making the dining experience way better for everyone.

By catching these trends early on, businesses can tackle issues before they snowball into something bigger. It's all about being proactive and making sure customers leave happy.

Real-Life Example: AI at Starbucks

Starbucks is really getting into the AI game with its Deep Brew system. It's like having a personal assistant for baristas! This smart tech helps them figure out what drinks are likely to be popular at different times, so they can keep everything stocked up just right. If you're someone who has a go-to drink, the app will even nudge you to order it as soon as you log in. It's pretty neat how this AI not only keeps your favorite latte on hand but also makes you feel like Starbucks really gets you. It's all about making your experience smoother and more personalized, which definitely keeps customers coming back for more.

Future of AI in Customer Service

AI is just getting started, and it's pretty exciting! As technology keeps moving forward, AI in customer service is going to get even better. Picture this: in the future, we could have virtual assistants that can chat with you just like a real person. They won't just remember your name; they'll keep track of all your past interactions, making every conversation feel seamless. Imagine chatting with a chatbot that not only helps you solve your problem but also knows your likes and dislikes from previous chats, making everything feel super smooth.

And it gets even better! We might see AI tools that can figure out what you need before you even ask for it. For example, if you're shopping online and tossing a pair of shoes into your cart, AI could pop up with suggestions for matching accessories or let you know about a sale on similar items. How handy is that? These features will make your shopping experience quick, efficient, and totally personalized.

AI is really shaking things up in customer service, making it faster, more tailored, and smarter with every interaction. From chatbots that are available 24/7 to personalized recommendations and voice recognition, AI is creating a world where businesses can meet your needs better than ever. As AI keeps evolving, the possibilities are endless, and we can look forward to even more cool innovations down the line. Whether you're shopping online, calling customer support, or chatting with a brand on social media, there's a good chance AI is working behind the scenes to make your experience smoother and way more enjoyable.

AI AND HR: RECRUITING AND ONBOARDING INNOVATIONS

In today's work scene, the Human Resources (HR) team is super important when it comes to hiring new folks, getting them settled in, and creating a great workplace vibe. Lately, Artificial Intelligence (AI) has become a go-to tool for HR pros, making their jobs a lot easier and more effective. It's like having a smart assistant that helps with everything from finding the right candidates to keeping employees happy and engaged. With AI's knack for sifting through huge amounts of data quickly and accurately, it's shaking up the way HR has traditionally operated. This means HR can now work smarter, tailoring their approaches to fit individual needs and making the whole process feel more personal. Overall, AI is really helping HR teams step up their game and create a better experience for everyone involved.

AI-Driven Recruitment Tools

Hiring has always felt more like an art than a science, but AI is changing the game. AI-powered recruitment tools are giving the hiring process a serious upgrade, taking over the tedious work—like sorting through resumes and matching candidates to job descriptions—so recruiters can focus on what really matters. These smart-systems don't just save time; they also reduce bias, ensuring candidates are evaluated fairly based on their skills and experience.

Beyond that, AI is revolutionizing recruitment with predictive analytics, helping companies identify candidates who are most likely to succeed. By analyzing past hiring decisions and employee performance, AI can pinpoint the traits and skills that lead to long-term success. For example, if a company finds that employees with specific skills or backgrounds thrive in certain roles, AI can prioritize candidates with similar profiles. This smarter, data-driven approach fills positions faster and helps build stronger, more cohesive teams.

Onboarding Personalization

The first few days at a new job are super important for how well employees do and how happy they feel. Nowadays, AI is stepping in to make the onboarding process way more effective by adding a personal touch. By looking at data from past successful onboarding experiences, AI helps HR managers create programs that fit the unique needs and learning styles of each new hire.

For example, some folks might really thrive with detailed technical training, while others might need a bit more help getting used to the company culture and working with their new team. Plus, AI-powered onboarding tools can take care of boring admin tasks like filling out paperwork and learning about company policies. This frees up HR professionals and managers to spend more time connecting with new hires and making them feel welcome.

These smart tools can also suggest personalized learning paths, pointing out training modules and resources that match employees' roles and career goals. This tailored approach not only makes onboarding more enjoyable for new hires but also helps them get up to speed faster, which is a win-win for both the employee and the company.

Employee Engagement Analysis

Keeping employees engaged is essential for maintaining a motivated and productive workforce. AI is making this process more effective by tracking engagement through pulse surveys, feedback tools, and mood-tracking apps. By continuously analyzing employee sentiments and satisfaction levels, AI helps HR teams gain valuable insights into workplace dynamics and areas that need improvement.

For example, if AI detects a drop in morale during particularly busy periods, HR can take proactive steps like adjusting team sizes, modifying project deadlines, or offering additional support to prevent burnout. Instead of reacting after issues arise, companies can address potential problems before they impact employee well-being and productivity.

AI also identifies patterns in engagement data, helping HR understand what keeps employees motivated, what factors contribute to stress, and what encourages long-term commitment. With these real-time insights, businesses can implement timely interventions, ensuring a positive and supportive work environment where employees feel valued and engaged.

Predictive Analytics in Employee Retention

Keeping your best employees is just as crucial as bringing in the right people in the first place, and guess what? AI can really help with that! By using predictive analytics, AI tools can take a good look at how employees interact, their performance reviews, and how engaged they are at work. This way, they can spot any signs that someone might be thinking about leaving. It's like having a crystal ball for employee retention.

This capability allows HR to proactively address factors contributing to employee turnover, such as:

- Career stagnation
- Work-life balance concerns
- Dissatisfaction with management or job responsibilities

AI can forecast which employees are at risk of leaving and pinpoint underlying issues, allowing HR to take proactive steps to improve retention. By analyzing patterns in employee behavior, feedback, and performance data, AI helps identify concerns before they lead to turnover. HR can then implement targeted retention strategies, such as:

- Offering career development opportunities
- Reevaluating workload and responsibilities

- Improving workplace policies and benefits

This proactive approach not only helps retain valuable employees but also reduces the significant costs associated with turnover, such as lost productivity and the expense of recruiting and training new hires.

The Expanding Role of AI in HR

AI is transforming HR by attracting talent, engaging employees, and enhancing retention. HR can streamline tasks and foster flexible workplaces, improving employee satisfaction and company culture. Ultimately, AI supports thriving, motivated workforces, making work better for all.

Conclusion: AI's Impact on Workplaces AI is reshaping workplaces by simplifying tasks and aiding strategic decision-making. Its ability to analyze vast data offers valuable insights, marking it as a pivotal asset across industries.

AI will increasingly shape our jobs. While challenges may arise, exciting opportunities await. Next, we'll explore AI's evolving role in the workplace and its impact across professions. Stay tuned for insights.

KNOWLEDGE CHECK: CHAPTER 4

1. Which of these AI applications is frequently used in marketing?
   A. AI-generated art
   B. Predictive analytics to forecast customer behavior
   C. Self-driving car software
   D. Natural Language Processing

2. Which AI tool can help project managers make better decisions?
   A. Autonomous robots
   B. AI-powered project management software
   C. AI-based customer service tools
   D. Machine learning for image recognition

3. **True or False:** AI can help companies streamline their hiring processes by using AI-driven tools to evaluate job candidates.
4. Short Answer

Describe one way AI can enhance business customer service.

Be the Hero Others Need!

Your Journey Can Spark Someone Else's Success!

Share Your AI Journey – Inspire Others!

You've tapped into some amazing insights about Artificial Intelligence, and now you have a great opportunity to share that knowledge with others. When you share your experience, it's more than just writing a review; you're creating a guide that can help someone else find the information that might change their life for the better.

Just think about it: your words could motivate someone to dive into the world of AI for the first time. Your thoughts might just be the nudge they need to kick off their own journey and reach their personal milestones. So, why not spread the word? Your perspective could be the inspiration someone else has been waiting for.

How You Can Make a Difference

Here's how you can be the hero that guides others to success:

- **Share Your Story:** What was your aha moment? Which part of this book had the biggest impact on you?
- **Inspire Others:** You've taken on AI—now help someone else feel confident enough to do the same.
- **Write a Quick Review:** You don't need to write an essay. Share how this book helped you and why others shouldn't miss out!

Take Action in Seconds!

Your story is worth sharing, and it's super easy to do:

- Leave a Review: Scan the QR code or click the link below.
- Share Your Experience: Help others unlock the same insights that made a difference for you.

It's quick, easy, and only takes a minute.

Scan the QR Code or Click here to leave a review to Share Your Thoughts.

Your Voice Matters

When you share your experience, you help not only the author but also future readers discover a resource that could change their lives.

Be the hero that someone else needs today. Your voice matters!

5

STAYING CURRENT WITH AI TRENDS

AI is evolving at lightning speed. Whether you're leveraging it at work or simply curious, staying updated is no longer optional. This chapter spotlights the breakthroughs shaping AI's future and why keeping up can give you a real edge.

TRACKING AI INNOVATIONS: KEY TRENDS TO WATCH

From quantum computing and AI ethics to the rise of augmented reality, new advancements are reshaping everything from business to daily life. Spotting these shifts early gives businesses, researchers, and developers a chance to adapt, innovate, and lead instead of playing catch-up.

Quantum Computing: The Next-Level Powerhouse

Quantum computing has shifted from a theoretical concept to a robust tool for tasks like drug discovery, financial modeling, and traffic management (Quantum Computing Journal, 2024). Unlike traditional machines, quantum systems harness superposition and entanglement to tackle challenges once deemed unsolvable (IBM Quantum, n.d.).

Staying informed about these breakthroughs means you'll be front-row for the next big leap in digital innovation.

AI Ethics & Accountability: Who's in Control?

AI is in everything from job-hiring tools to the movie suggestions you see online. But who ensures these systems stay fair and respect privacy? If bias slips in or data security fails, the fallout can be serious. That's why oversight and accountability matter. Whether a chatbot answers a quick question or a system screens job applicants, everyone deserves transparency and trust in each digital interaction (Smith & Johnson, 2024).

Augmented Reality (AR): Merging the Digital and Real Worlds

AR doesn't just power video games—it's transforming how we learn, shop, and even access medical care. When you keep track of AR's latest advances, you're ready to embrace tomorrow's possibilities. Whether you're a tech fan or just curious, AR is shaping everyday experiences in ways that once seemed like science fiction (Lee et al., 2023).

Staying Updated with the Right Tools

Tech Analysis Platforms:

- Sites like Gartner and TechCrunch dive deep into current AI trends, helping you see which technologies are more than just buzzwords. Gartner's Hype Cycles and Magic Quadrants, for example, highlight whether a tool or concept is truly poised for practical impact. If you're looking for clear, comprehensive insights, these are good places to start.

AI Newsletters & Publications:

- Weekly updates from MIT Technology Review or Jack Clark's Import AI can be a big help when you're busy. They gather new research findings in one spot and translate complex topics into readable summaries. It's an easy way to keep up with where AI is headed—minus the heavy technical jargon.

Regulatory Changes in AI

Governments around the globe are rolling out tighter regulations on data privacy, ethical AI use, and cross-border information sharing. The AI Governance Database and the OECD AI Policy Observatory are valuable resources to track these changes as they unfold. Staying in the loop helps organizations and everyday users respond quickly to new rules, preventing legal headaches and ensuring responsible AI practices.

Visual Element: Interactive AI Trend Tracker

For a more hands-on look at how AI is moving across different fields, consider an interactive tracker like Visual Capitalist. It offers real-time visual data, painting a clearer picture of AI's influence in diverse industries.

The Bottom Line

Following AI trends and using reliable resources can sharpen your skills and keep you relevant, whether you're learning for personal interest or career growth. It's about being proactive—diving into new tools, spotting opportunities, and staying agile in a world where AI isn't slowing down anytime soon.

PARTICIPATING IN AI CONFERENCES AND WEBINARS

Conferences give you a direct line to fresh ideas and seasoned experts. Before you sign up, pinpoint your goals—maybe you're there to learn about AI ethics, explore innovations in healthcare, or hone your technical skills. Plan out the sessions you'll attend, and come prepared with questions.

The Power of Networking

These events aren't just about listening; they're also your chance to meet like-minded people. Take a moment to introduce yourself to speakers and fellow attendees. Swap contact information, then follow up with a short, thoughtful message to keep the conversation going. One friendly chat can lead to future collaborations or job leads.

Virtual vs. In-Person Events: Choosing the Right Format

- **Virtual Conferences**: Typically cheaper and easier to fit into your day, though spontaneous meetups can be harder to come by.
- **In-Person Conferences:** These allow you to experience the buzz of a live audience and spark face-to-face conversations, but they can be pricier and may require travel.

When deciding between virtual and in-person, think about your budget, schedule, and priorities. If your goal is to network intensively, an in-person setting might be worth the extra time and cost. If you're focused on learning specific topics and have limited availability, online events could be a better fit.

Top AI Conferences to Attend

If you want to broaden your AI expertise, these events bring together top thinkers and cutting-edge discoveries:

- **NeurIPS**: Explores advanced neural networks and deep learning breakthroughs.
- **ICML**: Focuses on both theory and real-world applications in machine learning.
- **The AI Summit Series**: Highlights AI's impact on industries like healthcare and finance.
- **FAccT (Fairness, Accountability, and Transparency in AI)** focuses on ethical AI and responsible innovation.

Attending these conferences expands your knowledge and connects you with innovators in the field. This helps you sharpen your skills and stay current in a rapidly evolving landscape.

READING SCIENTIFIC PAPERS ON AI: A BEGINNER'S APPROACH

What's the Big Deal About Scientific Papers?

Scientific papers act like treasure maps, leading you toward new discoveries that power everything from AI to everyday tech. Sure, the language can feel heavy at first, but tackling it piece by piece makes it simpler. Highlight strange terms, look them up, and keep at it until the "muddy swamp" of jargon becomes more like a clear path. Each confusing part is simply a puzzle waiting to be solved, and every solution offers a fresh insight.

Start with Curiosity

Ask yourself what you really want to learn. Are you trying to figure out how AI identifies objects in images, or are you wondering how chatbots make sense of everyday language? Defining a clear question adds purpose to your reading.

For instance, if you're fascinated by how AI competes in games, search for papers on reinforcement learning—a key branch of AI dedicated to game strategy and decision-making. Having that focus makes finding papers that truly match your interests easier.

Choose Accessible Papers

Not all scientific papers are created equal—some are more approachable than others. Start with:

- Review articles or introductory papers that summarize broader AI topics. These provide a solid foundation and an excellent overview of the field.

- Open-access research papers that are available on platforms like Google Scholar, JSTOR, and IEEE Xplore.
- Papers that are written in clear, simple language. Some of the best researchers explain complex topics in an easy-to-understand way. Look for titles that include words like beginner or overview.

Interpreting Data and Results

When you finally get your hands on a paper, don't stress about trying to take in all the information at once. It's way more effective to tackle it piece by piece. Typically, scientific papers have a pretty standard layout, which makes it easier to navigate through them. So, just take your time and break it down into manageable sections. This way, you can really focus on understanding each part without feeling overwhelmed:

- **Abstract:** A summary of the entire paper. Read this first to get a quick overview of what to expect.
- **Introduction:** Explains why the research matters and sets the stage for what you'll learn.
- **Methods, Experiments, and Results:** This describes how the research was conducted and what was discovered. It can be technical, so focus on the main findings.
- **Discussion:** Connects the dots, explaining the significance of the research and how it relates to existing knowledge.
- **Conclusion:** Summarizes key findings and their impact, highlighting how the study contributes to AI research.

Take your time with each section. If you find unfamiliar terms, look them up! Many online resources, like YouTube, blogs, and AI tutorials, explain complex topics in a fun way.

Take Notes

As you read, jot down notes! Writing things down reinforces learning and helps you process complex ideas. Try this simple note-taking system:

- **Key Concepts:** Write down new terms and their definitions.
- **Questions:** Note any unclear points that need further research.
- **Personal Reflections:** Relate what you're learning to your interests. For example, if you love video games, consider how AI impacts game design.

Join the Conversation

Reading scientific papers can feel isolating, but it doesn't have to be! Engaging with others who share your interests can deepen your understanding. Here are some great ways to connect with fellow AI enthusiasts:

- **Forums:** Websites like Reddit have dedicated AI subreddits where people discuss papers, share resources, and ask questions. Don't be shy—jump in and participate!
- **Social Media:** Follow AI researchers and industry leaders on platforms like Twitter (X). Many share research insights, and you can interact by commenting or asking questions.
- **Online Courses:** Platforms like Coursera and edX offer AI courses with built-in discussion forums where you can exchange ideas with peers and instructors.

Keep It Real

While reading scientific papers is essential, don't forget to balance theory with practice!

- Watch documentaries about AI breakthroughs.
- Read news articles to stay updated on real-world applications of AI.

- Experiment with AI tools—platforms like Google's Teachable Machine let you create simple AI models without needing a computer science degree.

Engaging with real-world AI projects helps bridge the gap between theoretical knowledge and practical application.

Persevere

It's completely normal to feel overwhelmed by technical language or complex ideas when reading AI papers. Each small win—like cracking tough jargon or spotting a new angle—pushes you closer to understanding. The more papers you tackle, the more second nature they become. Here are a few tips:

- **Celebrate progress:** Acknowledge any new concept you grasp or interesting topic you discover.
- **Be patient:** Reading academic work is a skill that improves the more you practice.
- **Stay curious:** AI is an ever-evolving field, and fresh insights appear with every paper.

Reading AI research can feel like an exciting adventure. As you move forward:

- Let your questions guide you.
- Break papers into sections you can digest.
- Take notes to strengthen your recall.
- Connect with online communities for discussion.
- Apply new knowledge in real-world AI projects.

Above all, enjoy the ride—learning about AI should spark creativity, not just check a box.

THE FUTURE OF AI: PREDICTIONS AND PREPARATIONS

With AI weaving ever more deeply into our daily lives, it's natural to feel both energized and curious about what lies ahead. How might it transform our routines, reshape our work, or shift our thinking? Below are a few predictions on AI's future, along with tips on how to stay prepared in this fast-moving environment:

- **Growing Influence**: Expect AI to streamline tasks and uncover new solutions across industries.
- **Adaptation**: As AI adoption rises, learning basic concepts or acquiring AI-focused skills will help you remain agile at work and in everyday life.
- **Opportunity & Responsibility**: AI brings fresh possibilities but also demands thoughtful governance and ethical choices.

Exploring these developments equips you to handle new challenges and spot emerging opportunities—whether you're looking to innovate at work or simply stay informed as technology evolves.

The Rise of Smarter AI

A big thing to look forward to in the future is the development of super-smart AI systems. We're already seeing AI pop up in our daily lives—think about voice assistants that help us keep track of our schedules, recommendation systems that suggest what movies to watch, and algorithms that can even help diagnose health issues. But honestly, what's coming next is going to be even more impressive.

Picture this: an AI that can actually get a grip on human emotions learns from just a tiny bit of information and can adjust itself without needing a ton of programming. This is what we call general AI, and it would be able to tackle any intellectual task just like a human can. Researchers are pretty optimistic about making some serious progress in this field in the next few decades.

But here's the thing—while all these advancements sound amazing, it's super important to make sure we're using this technology ethically and responsibly as we move forward. We want to harness the power of AI without running into any major issues down the line.

AI in Every Industry

AI is not just for tech companies; it's transforming every industry. Here are a few areas where experts expect AI to impact significantly.

Healthcare

- AI is shaking things up in the world of healthcare, especially when it comes to diagnosing illnesses and planning treatments. Picture this: AI tools that can look at medical images and interpret them just as well as a seasoned radiologist. Plus, there are algorithms out there that can predict disease outbreaks by sifting through tons of data. These innovations are not just impressive; they're set to make a real difference in how patients are treated and how healthcare systems operate. With these advancements, we can expect better outcomes for patients and a smoother, more efficient healthcare experience overall.

Education

- AI is changing the way we learn by making it more personal and suited to each individual. Picture having a virtual tutor who really gets what you're struggling with and can offer you just the right resources to help you improve. This kind of approach could really open up opportunities for quality education all around the globe! It's exciting to think about how technology can make learning more accessible and tailored to everyone's unique journey.

Transportation

- Self-driving cars are just the start! Envision a future where AI enhances traffic management, reducing accidents and transforming public transport. Imagine streets where cars communicate with traffic signals for smooth, eco-friendly commutes.

Environment

- AI is a game-changer in combating climate change! It helps monitor the loss of forests, anticipate weather patterns, and optimize energy choices, empowering better decisions for our planet's health.

The Importance of Ethical AI

As AI systems evolve, it's crucial to ensure their responsible and ethical use. With great power comes great responsibility! Let's explore the key considerations for ethical AI development.

Transparency

- People must understand how AI makes decisions by developing algorithms that explain their reasoning. For example, if an AI denies a loan, it should provide clear reasons to avoid confusion and distrust.

Fairness

- AI systems must treat everyone fairly. Bias in AI can lead to discrimination in hiring and loans. Developers need to use diverse training data to ensure fair service for all.

Accountability

- AI accountability is crucial. If an AI system causes harm, identifying responsibility is essential. Developers, organizations, and policymakers must collaborate to establish clear guidelines and regulations to address these challenges effectively.

Preparing for the Future of AI

With all these changes on the horizon, how can we prepare for a future dominated by AI? Here are some strategies:

Continuous Learning

- AI is evolving super fast these days! If you want to keep up with all the changes, it's a great idea to embrace lifelong learning. There are tons of online courses, workshops, and community events out there that can help you stay in the loop with the newest trends and tools in the AI world. So, dive in and explore these resources—they can really make a difference in how you understand and interact with AI advancements.

Develop Soft Skills

- While technical skills are essential, soft skills like creativity, emotional intelligence, and critical thinking are equally important. AI cannot easily replicate these human skills and will set you apart in the future job market.

Embrace AI Tools

- Hey there! So, let's talk about some awesome AI tools that are made just for your industry. For instance, if you're in marketing, you can tap into how AI can boost your campaigns and give you some cool insights into what consumers are up to. Getting to know these tools is like gearing up for the future; trust me, it's worth it.

AI is opening up a ton of doors, from making our daily lives easier to sparking some seriously innovative ideas. But with all this potential, we've got to be mindful about how we develop it. It's super important that we all work together to make sure AI is used ethically so it can truly benefit everyone out there.

No matter if you're a student, a working professional, or just someone curious about the world, this is an exciting journey to be on! Keep that curiosity alive, keep learning new things, and remember, we're all in this together. Let's build a future where AI is not just a tool but a great partner in our growth and connections.

KNOWLEDGE CHECK: CHAPTER 5

1. What is one way to stay informed about the latest AI innovations?
   A. Attending AI conferences and webinars
   B. Ignoring AI research papers
   C. Relying solely on popular media
   D. Not participating in any online AI communities.
2. Which is a reliable source for learning more about AI advancements?
   A. Social media posts with no citations
   B. Peer-reviewed scientific papers
   C. AI memes
   D. Online shopping ads
3. **True or False:** Online AI communities, such as forums and social media groups, can provide valuable networking opportunities and access to the latest AI trends.
4. Short Answer:

Name one popular AI-related conference or webinar you could attend to stay current on trends.

6

HANDS-ON AI PROJECTS

Imagine stepping into a world where your ideas come to life—not just sitting on a page, but through interactions that think and respond. That's the fun of creating your own AI projects! It's all about taking what you've learned and turning it into real experiences, making AI something you don't just study but actively create and engage with.

This chapter will explore the exciting journey of building your first AI project: a chatbot. But don't think this is just about writing code; it's about bringing technology to life in a way that can chat, help out, and even entertain you.

Getting the hang of chatbots is a fantastic starting point, whether you want to make customer service smoother for a business or want to add something fun to your personal project lineup. So, let's dive in and see how you can turn your ideas into something that interacts with the world.

BUILDING YOUR FIRST CHATBOT

What is a Chatbot?

- A chatbot is a program that chats with you, kind of like having a conversation with a friend. You've likely come across them on various websites, where they pop up to help you out or guide you to the info you need. They're designed to make your online experience smoother, answering questions and providing support without you having to wait for a human to get back to you. It's pretty handy, right? Whether you're looking for help with a product or just need some quick info, these little digital assistants are there to lend a hand anytime you need it.
- Chatbots are built to understand what you say and respond in a way that feels helpful and human-like.

Why Build a Chatbot?

- Creating a chatbot is an excellent introduction to AI because it helps you understand how machines learn to respond to human language. Plus, it's a practical skill! Many businesses use chatbots to enhance customer service, making it a valuable tool to learn early on.

Getting Started: Free Tools for Chatbots

You don't need to start from scratch to build a chatbot. Here are a few beginner-friendly tools you can try:

- **Dialogflow (by Google):** This tool offers a free version and is great for beginners. It can understand and respond to natural language, meaning it can interpret what users are saying in their own words.

- **BotStar:** This tool is also beginner-friendly. It allows you to build interactive chatbots using drag-and-drop features. Students and educators can try BotStar for free.
- **ManyChat:** A popular platform for building Facebook Messenger bots. They offer a free version, so you can start experimenting right away.

Step-by-Step: Build a Basic Chatbot

- Let's walk through creating a simple chatbot using Dialogflow:
    - **Sign Up and Set Up**: Start by signing up for a free Dialogflow account. Once logged in, create a new Agent—essentially your chatbot's profile.
    - **Define Intents:** Intents determine how the chatbot understands user requests. For example, you can create an intent like Welcome, so your bot knows how to greet users. You'll need to provide example phrases for each intent.
    - **Set Responses:** Next, define how your chatbot should respond. You can add multiple response options to make it feel more natural and engaging. For example, "Hello! How can I assist you today?" or "Hi! What can I help you with?"
    - **Test and Improve:** Dialogflow lets you test your chatbot right away. After testing, you'll likely find areas where the bot needs improvement. For example, if users ask questions it doesn't understand, you can add new intents to handle those queries.

Fun Fact: Chatbots in the Real World

By 2025, chatbots are expected to handle 85% of customer service interactions! They provide faster responses than human agents and are available 24/7, making them a game-changer for businesses.

CREATING A SIMPLE RECOMMENDER SYSTEM

What is a Recommender System?

A recommender system is an AI-powered tool that helps you find new things you'll probably like. For instance, when you're binge-watching on Netflix, it's the system that pops up suggestions for shows you might like based on what you've already seen. Think about Spotify, which curates playlists and suggests songs that fit your taste. These systems are pretty clever; they analyze your preferences and behaviors to make educated guesses about what you might want to check out next. It's like having a personal assistant who knows your likes and dislikes, making it easier to find your next favorite movie or song without having to sift through endless options.

Why Build a Recommender System?

Getting a grip on recommender systems can really help you understand the inner workings of big names like Amazon, YouTube, and TikTok. These systems are not just fascinating; they also make for awesome projects if you're looking to dive into data handling, which is super important in the world of AI. Plus, working on these projects can give you invaluable hands-on experience. So, if you're curious about how these platforms suggest what you should check out next, learning about recommender systems is definitely the way to go.

Accessible Tools for Building a Recommender System

To start, try working with tools like:

- **Python**: Python is a programming language commonly used in AI. Free platforms like Google Colab allow you to code in Python online without installing anything.
- **Pandas and Scikit-Learn Libraries**: These libraries can help you analyze data. Both are free and powerful tools that AI enthusiasts use regularly.

Step-by-Step: Building a Basic Recommender System

Let's create a simple recommender system to recommend movies based on genre.

1. **Collect Data**: For this example, you'll need a dataset of movies with genres. Many free datasets are available online. Try Kaggle, a site where you can download free datasets on many topics.
2. **Data Analysis**: Use Python and the Pandas library to load your data. Look for patterns, such as grouping movies by genre.
3. **Build the Recommender**: Using Scikit-Learn, you can start with a simple similarity-based recommender. The system can recommend movies similar to those the user has rated highly.
4. **Testing and Adjusting**: Once you have your basic model, test it. Does it make sense? If it doesn't, adjust your data processing steps or try different algorithms in Scikit-Learn.

Fun Fact: How Spotify Knows Your Music Taste

Spotify's recommender system analyzes over 30 billion interactions between songs and users every day to create playlists that feel personal.

INTRODUCTION TO USING AI FOR BASIC IMAGE RECOGNITION

What is Image Recognition?

Image recognition is a fascinating branch of AI that helps computers figure out what's in pictures. Think about Google Photos—it can sort your images by recognizing faces, pets, and even where the photos were taken. This technology is a key player in the world of computer vision, which is super important for the advancements we see in AI today. It's amazing how these systems can learn to identify so many different things, making our lives a bit easier and more organized.

Whether it's tagging friends in photos or finding that perfect shot of your pet, image recognition definitely makes a mark in how we interact with our digital memories.

Why Try Image Recognition?

Image recognition projects are hands-on and help you see how AI can interpret the world visually. From recognizing cats and dogs to identifying different types of plants, you can experiment with this technology in endless ways.

Accessible Tools for Image Recognition

There are several free or low-cost tools to help you get started with image recognition:

- **Teachable Machine (by Google)**: This is a simple, web-based tool that allows you to train an image recognition model without any coding. It's perfect for younger students.
- **IBM Watson Studio**: IBM offers free-tier options for students. This is a more advanced tool that allows you to explore image recognition and other AI projects.
- **OpenCV and TensorFlow**: If you want to code your own image recognition project, Python libraries like OpenCV and TensorFlow are fantastic tools. Google Colab lets you access these for free in an online coding environment.

Step-by-Step: Create a Basic Image Recognition Model

Here's how to use Google's Teachable Machine for image recognition:

1. **Open Teachable Machine**: Go to Teachable Machine and click 'Get Started' to begin.
2. **Choose Image Project**: Select Image Project to begin building a model that recognizes objects in photos.
3. **Upload Images**: Take or upload photos of a few different

objects. For example, if you want to create a pet recognizer, upload images of cats and dogs.
4. **Train the Model**: Click **Train Model**, and the Teachable Machine will start learning to recognize your images. This usually takes a few minutes.
5. **Test and Improve**: Once your model is trained, you can test it live. If it doesn't work well, add more images or take clearer photos.

Real-World Uses of Image Recognition

Image recognition is a pretty handy tool these days, popping up in areas like security, healthcare, and even social media. Take Facebook, for example; it's got this feature that suggests friends you might want to tag in your photos, making it easier to share those memories. On the healthcare side, hospitals are getting involved in the action, too. They can use image recognition technology to help spot diseases by analyzing medical scans, which is a big deal for improving patient care. It's fascinating to see how this tech is making life a bit simpler and more efficient in various fields.

Ethical AI Use: Why It's Important

As you explore AI, remember that ethical use is essential. For instance:

- Always give credit for any data or tools you use.
    - Be transparent about how you gather information, especially if it involves images or personal data.
    - Avoid copying code or projects that are precisely from someone else. Make it your own!

Exploring AI through these projects is a fun way to learn about technology that shapes our world. Whether you're chatting with a chatbot, discovering new music recommendations, or identifying objects in photos, you're experiencing the power of AI. As you work on these projects, remember that AI is about creativity and problem-solving.

Keep experimenting, and let your imagination guide you. Who knows? One day, you might create the next big thing in AI!

UNLEASHING AI IN MUSIC AND SOCIAL MEDIA

AI in Music and Social Media: Creative and Analytical Applications

AI has become a creative powerhouse, helping artists compose music and enabling businesses to analyze social media sentiments. In this chapter, we'll explore how AI can generate music and interpret social media trends. These projects are accessible, engaging, and perfect for young learners interested in using AI for creative and analytical purposes.

AI in Music: Composing with AI Tools

What Does It Mean to Compose Music with AI?

- Composing music with AI involves using algorithms and machine learning models to create original compositions or enhance existing pieces.
- AI can recognize patterns in different types of music, making it possible to generate melodies, harmonies, and even entire songs.
- AI music tools analyze elements such as rhythm, pitch, and tempo and use these patterns to create new musical ideas.

Why Compose Music with AI?

- **Experimentation:** AI allows you to explore different sounds and styles without needing advanced music theory knowledge.
- **Creativity:** It's a great way to quickly bring musical ideas to life, especially if you're curious about experimenting with various genres and unique compositions.

- **Accessibility:** AI music tools make composition easier, providing an entry point for beginners and experienced musicians alike.

Tools for Composing Music with AI

Several free and trial-based tools make composing music with AI easy and fun:

- **AIVA (Artificial Intelligence Virtual Artist)** – Specializes in composing classical music and other genres. It offers a free tier, making it an excellent tool for experimenting with AI-generated compositions.
- **Magenta Studio by Google** – A set of music plugins that work with software like Ableton Live. Magenta is free and open-source, making it an excellent choice for those interested in music generation and AI exploration.
- **Boomy** – A user-friendly AI music tool that lets you create full songs in various genres with just a few clicks. It offers a free plan, making it great for beginners and casual users looking to experiment with AI-generated music.

Step-by-Step: Compose Music with AIVA

Let's walk through composing a simple piece of music using AIVA:

1. **Sign Up and Set Up**: Start by signing up for a free AIVA account. Once you're in, you can select the Create New Composition option.
2. **Choose a Style**: AIVA lets you select the style of music you want to compose, from classical to pop. Choose a genre and set the mood for your piece.
3. **Customize Instruments**: You can pick the instruments you'd like AIVA to use, such as piano, strings, or percussion. This is where you start shaping the sound.

4. **Generate and Refine**: Click Generate to let AIVA create a melody. You can listen to the results and make adjustments. AIVA allows you to edit the piece to change the tempo or add another instrument.
5. **Download and Share**: Once you're satisfied, you can download your music as an audio file to share with friends or use in a project.

Fun Fact: AI in the Music Industry

- AI is used not only for composing but also to enhance music production. For example, Sony's Flow Machines project used AI to help produce Daddy's Car, a song inspired by The Beatles. This shows how AI can be part of the creative process in mainstream music.

ANALYZING SOCIAL MEDIA SENTIMENTS WITH AI

What is Sentiment Analysis?

- Sentiment analysis is a cool AI process that helps determine what people say in their texts, especially on social media. It sorts opinions into three categories: positive, negative, or neutral. By checking out social media posts, companies can get a feel for how folks react to their products, brands, or services. This kind of analysis is super helpful for businesses because it gives them a better understanding of their customers. With this insight, they can make smarter, data-driven choices that really resonate with their audience. It's all about tuning in to what people think and feel.

Why Use AI for Social Media Sentiment Analysis?

- With millions of tweets, Instagram comments, and Facebook posts shared every day, it's impossible for people to keep track

of everyone's thoughts and feelings. AI can analyze this information quickly and at scale, providing valuable insights into public opinion.
- Tools for Social Media Sentiment Analysis

There are several tools available—many of which offer free or trial versions—to help you get started with sentiment analysis:

- **MonkeyLearn:** A user-friendly, no-code tool with a free version. MonkeyLearn allows you to analyze text for sentiment, categorizing it as positive, negative, or neutral.
- **Hugging Face's Transformers Library:** If you're interested in coding, this Python library provides pre-trained models for sentiment analysis. It is free to use on Google Colab.
- **Google Sheets with Sentiment Analysis Add-Ons:** Some Google Sheets add-ons can analyze text sentiment, making this a great option for those who prefer working in a spreadsheet environment.

Step-by-Step: Analyzing Sentiment with MonkeyLearn

Let's walk through analyzing tweets or social media comments using MonkeyLearn:

1. **Sign Up and Set Up:** Create a free MonkeyLearn account. Once signed up, you'll have access to the dashboard.
2. **Create a New Model:** MonkeyLearn offers pre-trained models for sentiment analysis, but you can also train your own by feeding it examples of positive, negative, and neutral comments.
3. **Import Data:** Upload a list of comments or posts from a CSV file or paste them directly into MonkeyLearn.
4. **Analyze Sentiments:** MonkeyLearn processes each text entry and classifies it as positive, negative, or neutral. It also

provides a confidence score, indicating how sure the model is about each classification.
5. **Visualize the Results:** MonkeyLearn allows you to view the results in different formats, such as charts and tables, making it easy to interpret the overall sentiment in your dataset.

Real-World Use: Sentiment Analysis in Marketing

Companies like Starbucks and Nike are getting into the groove of using sentiment analysis to keep tabs on what customers say about them on social media. By diving into those social media mentions, these brands can catch onto trends, manage their image, and quickly tackle any customer issues that pop up. It's pretty impressive that around 75% of companies are now using AI to interact with customers in some way, and sentiment analysis is a big player in helping shape their marketing strategies. This approach helps them understand their audience better and allows them to respond in real-time, making the whole experience smoother for everyone involved.

Ethical Use of AI in Creative and Analytical Projects

When working with AI, it's essential to be mindful of ethical considerations:

- **Transparency**: Always tell others if your music or analysis was AI-assisted. This builds trust and ensures credit is given where it's due.
- **Data Privacy**: Avoid using sensitive information and be cautious with personal data for sentiment analysis. Ensure you're only working with publicly available or anonymized data.
- **Originality in Music**: Although AI can help you create music, adding your unique touch is essential. Try to adjust the AI-generated piece to reflect your personal style or taste.

AI is an incredible tool that can shake things up in creative and analytical fields. Whether you're jamming out a new song or diving into what people are saying on social media, AI helps you turn all that data into something that makes sense. As you dive into these projects, remember that AI is all about trying new things and learning along the way. So, go ahead and have a blast creating, analyzing, and uncovering all the exciting possibilities that AI has to offer.

The Beginners Step-by-Step Hands-on Practice Exercises can be downloaded here. Click the link or scan the QR code to download AI Essentials: Tools, Exercises & Resources.

AI Essentials: Tools, Exercises, and Resources

KNOWLEDGE CHECK: CHAPTER 6

1. Which platform is commonly used to build simple chatbots?
    A. TensorFlow
    B. Dialogflow
    C. PyTorch
    D. MATLAB
2. Which AI project involves recommending items to users based on their past preferences?
    A. Image recognition
    B. Recommender system
    C. AI-powered chatbots
    D. Virtual reality
3. **True or False:** Sentiment analysis using AI can apply to social media to understand public opinions about a brand.
4. Short Answer:

Describe the key steps involved in building a simple chatbot.

7

ETHICAL AI USE AND CONSIDERATIONS

Artificial Intelligence (AI) has become a part of our everyday lives, influencing everything from amazing medical advancements to the gadgets we use daily. It's pretty wild to think about how much it's integrated into what we do. But with all these exciting possibilities, we also have to face some tough questions that are important to consider. What does this mean for our future? How do we navigate the challenges that come with such rapid change? It's a lot to think about.

- Is AI being fair?
- Are we giving up too much of our privacy?
- And who's responsible when things go wrong?
- These aren't abstract debates but real issues shaping our present and future.

Let's examine where ethics meet AI and why it matters to everyone.

UNDERSTANDING AI BIAS AND HOW TO MITIGATE IT

AI systems might look neutral, but they're only as fair as the data they learn from. And since that data usually comes from us humans—who are far from perfect and carry our own biases—AI can pick up and even magnify those biases without meaning to.

Take a company that uses AI to sift through job applications, for instance. If the AI is trained on data showing that most executives are men, it could give a leg up to male candidates while completely ignoring equally qualified women or people from underrepresented backgrounds.

This whole situation, which we call AI bias, isn't just a tech problem; it pops up in all sorts of fields like criminal justice, healthcare, and even the algorithms that decide what you see on social media. A study from MIT back in 2018 showed that facial recognition tech had a tough time with Black women, misidentifying them 34% of the time, while it only messed up 1% of the time with white men. These aren't just minor hiccups; they have serious real-life impacts, affecting people's jobs, lives, and their access to crucial services. It's a big deal that we need to pay attention to.

Bias and Discrimination in AI

When AI absorbs biases from its training data, it can lead to:

- Unfair Treatment: Certain groups may face barriers to employment, loans, or healthcare.
- Discriminatory Decisions: AI may reinforce stereotypes, favoring some individuals while unintentionally excluding others.

When it comes to hiring, let's think about how AI can sometimes miss the mark. If the AI is trained on biased data, it might end up favoring candidates from certain backgrounds while overlooking others who could be just as qualified, if not more so. This isn't just a problem in hiring; it also pops up in healthcare. AI systems can struggle to provide the same level of care for underrepresented groups, which only makes the existing inequalities worse. It's a real issue that needs attention, as it affects opportunities and outcomes for many people.

AI's Impact on Employment

While AI boosts productivity and streamlines tasks, it also raises concerns about job displacement. Automation is rapidly transforming industries, with its effects most visible in:

- **Manufacturing:** Machines are taking over repetitive, labor-intensive tasks on assembly lines.
- **Customer Service:** AI-powered chatbots are replacing entry-level positions, handling customer inquiries 24/7.
- **Administrative Work:** AI automates data entry, scheduling, and other routine tasks, reducing the need for human employees.

The Ethical Question: What Happens to Workers Left Behind?

As automation advances, reskilling programs for workers losing jobs are crucial. These initiatives help individuals transition to new roles. However, the alarming job losses raise concerns about whether new opportunities will emerge to offset this. It's a complex situation that requires careful monitoring.

How to Mitigate AI Bias

Fixing AI bias is challenging but not impossible. Here are three critical steps to create fairer AI systems:

- **Train on Diverse Data:** The more representative the data, the fairer the results. AI trained on data that includes varied genders, races, and backgrounds is less likely to perpetuate old biases.

- **Conduct Regular Audits:** AI systems need frequent reviews to detect and correct biased outcomes. Think of this as giving AI a routine checkup to ensure it remains fair.
- **Be Transparent:** Companies must clearly explain how their AI systems work and what data they use. Openness builds trust and allows external experts to help identify problems.

AI is really just a tool we get to mold and shape; it doesn't just run independently. It's up to all of us—whether you're a developer, part of a corporation, a government official, or an everyday person—to ensure that it's fair and just. If we stay alert and put in the effort, AI has the potential to be something that brings us together instead of tearing us apart.

PRIVACY CONCERNS WITH AI TECHNOLOGIES

AI is super hungry for data—think about all the little bits of info we leave behind every day, like our clicks, locations, and chats. Whenever you ask a virtual assistant for directions, scroll through your social media, or adjust your smart thermostat, you're dropping the breadcrumbs of your life in data. From daily routines to health details, this data fuels AI systems. But how safe is it? Who's ensuring it's used responsibly? And what exactly is being collected?

From the moment you interact with AI, vast amounts of personal data are being logged, such as:

- **Where You Are:** Location tracking pinpoints your movements in real-time.
- **What You Do:** Devices monitor your routines, like when you wake up or adjust your thermostat.
- **Who You Are:** Health trackers and apps record sensitive details about your body and habits.

Smart home systems, such as Google Nest, have this amazing ability to learn your habits and create detailed profiles about your daily life. While having this kind of insight is super handy, it raises some concerns. Many people might not realize how their data is being used or who gets to see it. It's a bit of a double-edged sword—convenience on one side, but potential privacy issues on the other. So, while these gadgets can make life easier, staying aware of what's happening behind the scenes with your information is essential.

The Risks of Data Collection

AI's reliance on personal data raises some serious concerns:

- **Exploitation of Information:** Companies often mishandle gathered data. A prime example is the Facebook and Cambridge Analytica incident, where millions of users' personal information was exploited to influence political campaigns. This raises concerns about how carefully companies protect our data and the activities happening in the background. We must remain vigilant and safeguard our information in today's data-driven world.
    - **Surveillance on a Large Scale:** Governments and companies are adopting AI for surveillance. For instance, China uses facial recognition to monitor citizens, raising concerns about personal freedom. This issue highlights technology's impact on privacy and prompts questions about the limits of surveillance and its implications for individuals' rights.
    - **Data Breaches:** Storing more data increases the risk of theft. The 2017 Equifax breach exposed the private information of over 140 million Americans, highlighting that even secure systems are vulnerable. This serves as a reminder to protect our personal information—no system is entirely foolproof.

Guarding Your Privacy

In the digital age, protecting personal information requires action on both individual and systemic levels. Here are some critical steps:

- **Strengthen Regulations:** Laws like the EU's General Data Protection Regulation (GDPR) provide a blueprint for giving users control over their data and ensuring companies handle it transparently.
    - **Embrace Encryption:** Encrypting data adds a layer of security, making it harder for hackers to access sensitive information. Companies like Apple have led the charge by implementing stronger device encryption.
    - **Stay Informed:** As users, we must proactively understand what we share and with whom. Simple steps like reading privacy settings, limiting app permissions, and using tools like VPNs (virtual private networks) can significantly safeguard your online activity.

AI is powerful but has a big appetite for data, which has downsides. Privacy is about controlling your information. While AI makes life easier, we must be careful about the personal information we share. Protecting our privacy in this AI-driven world is a collective responsibility. Let's be smart and avoid handing over our data thoughtlessly.

THE SOCIETAL IMPACT OF AI: A BALANCED VIEW

Artificial Intelligence (AI) is changing how we live, exciting yet nerve-wracking. It's everywhere, transforming businesses and raising ethical questions. We can't overlook its influence. Let's explore how AI impacts our lives, the opportunities it creates, and the challenges ahead. There's a lot to unpack, and it's worth discussing!

Autonomy and Control

As AI handles our schedules and finances, the line between convenience and dependence blurs. Automated tasks reduce our engagement in decision-making.

For example:

- **AI Assistants:** Helpful for reminders and organization, but over-reliance could dull our decision-making instincts.
- **Automation in Daily Life:** From grocery deliveries to financial planning, the increasing use of AI shifts responsibility away from individuals, creating a subtle dependency on technology.

While AI enhances efficiency, it raises an important question: Are we handing over too much control to systems we don't fully understand?

Security Risks

AI systems—especially those connected to the internet—are attractive targets for hackers. When compromised, the consequences can be severe:

- Personal Data Theft: Sensitive information, from passwords to financial records, can be exposed.
- Device Takeover: Hackers could gain control over smart home devices, including security cameras and thermostats.
- Critical Infrastructure Threats: AI vulnerabilities in power grids or transportation systems could significantly disrupt essential services.

To mitigate these risks, robust security measures—such as encryption and regular system updates—are essential. However, ensuring these protections requires vigilance from both users and developers.

Ethical Use of AI in Healthcare

AI is transforming healthcare, but its rapid adoption raises critical ethical questions:

- **Informed Patients:** Patients must understand how AI influences their care. If an algorithm suggests a treatment,

patients have the right to know the reasoning behind that recommendation.
- **Retaining Control:** Patients should always have the final say in their medical decisions, even as AI becomes a more significant part of the process.

Without clear communication, AI-driven healthcare decisions risk alienating patients, making them feel uncertain or mistrustful of their treatment.

Positive Impacts of AI

AI's potential to improve society is immense, especially in fields like:

- **Healthcare:** Systems like IBM's Watson analyze vast datasets to assist in diagnosing diseases such as cancer. AI also predicts outbreaks, enabling quicker, more effective responses.
- **Education:** AI-powered platforms personalize learning experiences, adapting content to each student's pace and style —making education more accessible and practical.
- Environment: AI helps optimize energy use in data centers, enables farmers to predict weather and boost crop yields, and contributes to combating climate change through sustainable innovations.

Negative Impacts of AI

Despite its benefits, AI also presents challenges that require careful consideration:

- **Job Displacement:** Automation threatens millions of jobs in manufacturing, customer service, and even medicine. A McKinsey report estimates that up to 375 million jobs could be automated by 2030, highlighting the urgent need for workforce retraining.

- **Social Media Echo Chambers:** AI-driven algorithms on platforms like Facebook and Twitter often prioritize content users already agree with, reinforcing echo chambers that amplify misinformation and deepen societal divides.
- **AI in Warfare:** The use of autonomous weapons raises troubling ethical concerns. Drones and AI-driven military systems, capable of operating without human intervention, pose serious questions about accountability and unintended harm.

Finding Balance

AI's power to reshape society comes with immense responsibility. To ensure AI benefits everyone, we must address its risks while thoughtfully embracing its opportunities.

Governments, tech companies, and individuals all have roles to play, whether by:

- Developing fair and unbiased AI systems
- Protecting user privacy
- Holding developers accountable for ethical considerations

AI's promise is vast, but so are its challenges. By balancing progress with caution, we can harness its potential to improve lives while upholding the human values that matter most.

DEVELOPING TRANSPARENT AI SYSTEMS

Transparency in AI: Why It Matters and How to Achieve It

Being transparent with AI means ensuring its systems and decisions are clear and understandable. It seems simple, but it isn't very easy. Many AI systems, especially deep learning ones, are like mysterious black boxes. Their workings are so intricate that even experts struggle to understand their conclusions. Whether AI recommends a show or aids in diagnosing a health issue, understanding the reasoning behind decisions is crucial for building trust and improving interaction technologies.

The Double-Edged Sword of Transparency and Accountability

AI systems functioning as black boxes pose significant challenges:

- **Hidden Decision-Making:** The reasoning behind decisions like loan approvals and facial recognition typically involves complex algorithms with multiple layers, making their logic challenging to understand.
- **Lack of Accountability:** When mistakes occur—such as wrongful arrests based on faulty AI—it's hard to pinpoint where or why the system went wrong. This lack of clarity complicates efforts to assign responsibility, leaving affected individuals in a frustrating limbo.

Why Transparency is Non-Negotiable

1. **Trust-Building:** People feel more comfortable trusting AI when its reasoning is clear. For example, if someone is denied a bank loan, it's crucial to know why—was it their credit score, income, or something else? When systems are transparent about these details, trust is built. People value straightforward answers to questions, making the experience more transparent and intimidating.
2. Accountability: When AI causes harm, transparency allows developers to trace errors, diagnose the issue, and implement fixes. Without a clear understanding of the system's logic, errors can remain unresolved, leading to repeated failures.
3. Regulatory Compliance: Laws such as the EU's General Data Protection Regulation (GDPR) demand transparency, granting individuals explanations for AI decisions that impact their lives. To comply, systems must be transparent by design.

How to Develop Transparent AI Systems

Achieving transparency in AI is no small task, but these strategies can make a significant difference:

1. Explainable AI (XAI): Create systems that explain their decisions straightforwardly. For instance, if a medical AI suggests a treatment plan, it should clearly define which test results or symptoms influenced its choice and reasoning.
2. Open-Source Models: Sharing code and datasets for AI fosters collaboration and transparency. For instance, OpenAI has made several models public, allowing researchers and developers to improve them and learn new skills.
3. Simplified User Interfaces: Even if the underlying technology is complex, presenting findings through easy-to-read visuals—such as graphs, flowcharts, or interactive dashboards—makes AI systems more accessible to non-experts. Clear explanations ensure that users feel informed rather than intimidated.

A Path to Ethical AI

Transparency is essential for ethical AI development. By clarifying AI systems, developers can create practical tools that build trust. Ensuring transparency allows AI to collaborate with us, fostering a future where technology supports human needs and values.

ETHICAL AI DESIGN AND DEVELOPMENT PRACTICES

Designing ethical AI goes beyond checking boxes—ensuring fairness, human rights, and privacy. AI now influences areas like hiring and healthcare, so developing it ethically is crucial to benefit everyone, not just a select few.

Ethics in AI Development

With great power comes significant responsibility. For AI developers, this means treating ethics not as an afterthought but as the foundation of their work. Ensuring transparency, safeguarding privacy, and respecting intellectual contributions aren't optional—they're essential.

Here's how developers can lead by example:

- **Transparency:** Inform users about how their data will be used. If you're building a recommendation system, explain the logic behind it.
- **Privacy Protection:** Personal data, like medical records or financial information, should always be anonymized and handled carefully.
- **Credit Where It's Due:** To avoid plagiarism and support a collaborative ecosystem, open-source tools, datasets, and code must be appropriately cited.

Respecting these principles builds trust and aligns with regulations like the European Union's GDPR, which enforces strict data protection standards.

Why Does Ethical AI Design Matter?

1. **Preventing Harm:** Poorly designed AI can cause real-world damage, such as perpetuating inequality in hiring systems through biased algorithms.
2. **Preserving Human Rights:** Systems must honor fundamental rights like privacy, freedom, and equality. For instance, surveillance tools should not be used to target individuals or monitor them unfairly without their consent.
3. **Maintaining Trust:** Public confidence is critical as AI takes on roles in sensitive areas like finance or law enforcement. Ethically designed systems are more likely to earn and sustain trust.

Principles of Ethical AI Design

To ensure AI systems are fair and responsible, developers should follow these five guiding principles:

1. **Fairness:** Design systems that treat everyone equally. This includes using diverse datasets to minimize bias and tools that identify and reduce algorithmic bias.
    - *Example:* Bias detection tools analyze AI models to ensure they don't disproportionately disadvantage specific demographics.
2. **Accountability:** Developers must take responsibility for their systems' actions. This means establishing safeguards and transparent processes for addressing errors or harm.
    - *Example:* Tesla's challenges with accidents involving self-driving cars highlight the need for accountability frameworks in AI-driven technologies.
3. **Privacy Protection:** Ethical AI minimizes data collection, anonymizes information, and only gathers what's strictly necessary.
    - *Example:* Companies like Apple are raising the bar with stricter privacy features, ensuring users' data isn't shared without explicit consent.
4. **Transparency:** Users have the right to understand how AI systems function and make decisions. Simple, clear explanations foster trust and allow users to challenge decisions when necessary.
5. **Human-Centered Design:** Technology should enhance human decision-making rather than replace it entirely.
    - *Example:* AI-powered medical tools assist doctors by quickly analyzing data, but final treatment decisions remain in the hands of healthcare professionals.

Ethical AI in Action

Some organizations are setting the standard for ethical AI practices:

- **Google:** In 2018, Google introduced principles to guide its AI development, focusing on avoiding harm, ensuring fairness, and rejecting applications for surveillance or weaponry.
- **European Commission:** The EU's Ethics Guidelines for Trustworthy AI promote fairness, privacy, and long-term societal impact.
- **IBM:** IBM's AI Fairness 360 toolkit helps developers identify and reduce bias in AI models, supporting fairness in critical fields like hiring and healthcare.

Challenges and the Road Ahead

Creating ethical AI poses challenges. As systems grow complex, ensuring fairness and transparency becomes harder. Some developers may overlook ethics for profit or speed.

Moving forward requires collaboration between governments, developers, and users:

- **Education and Training:** Equip future AI professionals with the tools to recognize and address ethical challenges.
- **Adaptive Regulations:** As AI evolves, laws must keep pace with new technologies and potential risks.

The future of AI relies on merging technological advancements with ethics. By prioritizing fairness, openness, and consideration, we can ensure that AI truly benefits society. Trust is essential for good AI and holds everything together.

KNOWLEDGE CHECK: CHAPTER 7

1. **What is one of the main concerns regarding AI bias?**
   A. AI can perfectly replicate human thinking.
   B. AI can make biased decisions based on the data it is trained on.
   C. AI always makes fair and unbiased decisions.
   D. AI systems are never impacted by bias.
2. **Which of the following is a key privacy concern with AI?**
   A. AI does not store any data.
   B. AI systems can collect and use personal data without consent.
   C. AI systems can only access publicly available information.
   D. AI is entirely transparent about its use of data.
3. **True or False:** It is crucial to design AI systems that are transparent and explainable to minimize ethical concerns.
4. **Short Answer:**

How can organizations reduce bias in their AI systems?

8

CAREER PATHS IN AI

AI isn't just about coding or building robots. The world of AI has many jobs, each needing its own skills. Let's check out some of the leading roles you might find in the AI field.

EXPLORING AI JOB ROLES AND REQUIRED SKILLS

AI Research Scientist:

- These people are at the forefront of AI innovation. They're focused on creating algorithms that enable machines to learn and think independently. An AI research scientist gets into the nitty-gritty of advanced math, algorithms, and machine learning (ML). They also conduct experiments to develop new AI techniques.
- **Key Skills**: Deep learning, machine learning algorithms, programming (Python, TensorFlow), statistical analysis.
  - **Fun Fact**: Did you know that in 2023, an AI research scientist in the U.S. earned an average salary of over $130,000 a year?

Data Scientist:

- AI revolves around data, and data scientists dive into those tricky datasets to find insights that aid in making decisions. In AI projects, they build models that can forecast what might happen next or enhance processes, like recommending the next video you'd love to watch on YouTube.
- **Key Skills**: Data analysis, statistical modeling, machine learning, and data visualization (using tools like Matplotlib or Seaborn).
    - **Real-World Example**: Companies like Google and Amazon hire hundreds of data scientists to improve customer experience and optimize operations.

Machine Learning Engineer:

- Machine learning engineers build and train AI models to ensure they run efficiently with large data. Their role combines software engineering and machine learning, involving algorithm design, model fine-tuning, and performance optimization. They improve data pipelines, select tools, and ensure scalable AI solutions. With technical skills and problem-solving they are essential in developing AI systems powering recommendation engines and self-driving cars.
- **Key Skills**: Programming (Python, R), deep learning, neural networks, cloud computing.
    - **Real World Example**: If you've ever used Google Translate, you've seen a machine learning model in action. It's machine learning engineers who develop these models.

AI Ethics Officers:

- AI Ethics Officers are crucial in ensuring AI is used fairly and transparently. They work to reduce algorithm bias, protect user privacy, and uphold ethical guidelines. Their responsibilities

include reviewing data sources, setting policies, and collaborating with developers to create unbiased models. By prioritizing ethics, they foster trust in AI and ensure technology benefits everyone.
- **Key Skills:** AI knowledge, ethics, data privacy, and communication.
  - **Important Note:** Transparency and ethical AI use are vital as systems make life-altering decisions, like facial recognition or credit scoring.

Robotics Engineer:

- Robotics engineers design and build machines that can carry out tasks autonomously, often using AI. They work on everything from manufacturing robots to autonomous vehicles.
- **Key Skills**: Mechanical engineering, programming, AI algorithms, hardware integration.
  - **Fun Fact**: The global robotics market was valued at over $23 billion in 2021 and is expected to grow significantly in the next decade.

AI Product Manager:

- AI product managers oversee the development and deployment of AI-driven products. They coordinate teams and ensure that AI applications align with business goals and user needs.
- **Key Skills**: Project management, AI technologies, communication, business strategy.
  - **Real World Example**: AI product managers at companies like Tesla work to make autonomous driving a reality.

HOW TO TRANSITION TO A CAREER IN AI

Switching to a career in AI might seem daunting, especially if you come from a non-technical background. However, with determination and a well-structured plan, it's achievable.

Step 1: Identify Your Interests

AI has many subfields, including natural language processing, computer vision, and robotics. Research these areas to identify what interests you most.

- Do you enjoy working with data?
- Are you more interested in developing algorithms?
- Finding your niche will help guide your learning path and focus your efforts.

Step 2: Learn the Basics

A strong foundation in AI involves learning programming and key mathematical concepts. Here are some essential skills to acquire:

- **Programming:** Start with Python, the most popular language in AI due to its simplicity and extensive libraries like TensorFlow and Keras.
- **Mathematics:** Brush up on linear algebra, probability, and statistics, which are crucial for understanding machine learning algorithms.
- There are plenty of free online resources available. Platforms like Coursera, edX, and Khan Academy offer courses in programming and AI.
- **Tip:** You don't need to be an expert from day one—focus on gradually building your skills.

Step 3: Gain Hands-On Experience

- While theory is important, practical experience is essential.
- Start with small projects. You can find datasets on platforms like Kaggle to practice building machine learning models.
- Create a GitHub repository to showcase your projects. Having a portfolio will be valuable when applying for jobs.
- **Tip:** Employers look for real-world experience, so demonstrating your ability to apply AI concepts is key.

Step 4: Get a Certification or Degree

- Many folks manage to dive into AI by teaching themselves, but getting a formal education can help, especially if you're from a non-tech background.
- You can pursue a master's degree in AI or a related field.
- Alternatively, many reputable institutions offer online AI certifications, which employers recognize and can enhance your credentials.

Step 5: Network and Join AI Communities

- AI is changing fast, and it's super helpful to connect with others who are into it, too. This way, you can stay in the loop with all the new trends and developments.
- Attend conferences, participate in online forums, and engage with AI communities.
- LinkedIn groups and Reddit's r/MachineLearning are great places to connect with others and learn insights from pros in the field.

SKILLS DEVELOPMENT: FROM NOVICE TO AI EXPERT

Transitioning from a beginner to an AI expert is a journey. Here's a step-by-step guide to developing your skills.

Beginner Level: Building the Foundation

- **Focus Areas:** Programming (Python), basic statistics, and an introduction to AI concepts (supervised and unsupervised learning).
- **Resources:** Beginner-friendly courses such as Coursera's AI for Everyone by Andrew Ng or Python for Data Science by DataCamp.

Intermediate Level: Applying AI Techniques

- **Focus Areas:** Machine learning algorithms (linear regression, decision trees), neural networks, and data preprocessing.
- **Practice:** Work on projects using real-world datasets—for example, build a recommendation engine or create a chatbot.
- **Tip:** Participate in AI hackathons or Kaggle competitions to sharpen your skills and gain hands-on experience.

Advanced Level: Mastering AI Specializations

- **Focus Areas:** Deep learning, reinforcement learning, natural language processing (NLP), and AI ethics.
- **Hands-On Projects:** Work on complex projects such as image classification models or natural language generation models.
- **Tip:** Stay updated on new AI research by reading papers on platforms like arXiv and attending AI conferences.

Expert Level: Innovating in AI

- **Focus Areas:** Cutting-edge AI research, advanced machine learning techniques, and AI leadership roles.
- **Contribute to the Field:** By this stage, aim to contribute to AI research, publish findings, or mentor others in the field.
- **Fun Fact:** Google's DeepMind and OpenAI are two research institutions known for leading AI innovations, such as AlphaGo and GPT-3.

AI is transforming industries and our lives. As you explore AI, remember it's a journey of learning and growth, not instant expertise. Whether you aspire to be an AI research scientist or a product manager, there's a place for you in AI.

Focus on ethical AI, enhance your skills, and stay curious to make an impact. AI presents opportunities for creative thinkers and problem solvers. Take the first step to creating the next big thing by mastering your technical skills. Remember to build connections and earn relevant certifications.

To stand out in AI, networking and continuous education are essential.

NETWORKING AND BUILDING PROFESSIONAL RELATIONSHIPS IN AI

Networking in AI involves connecting with people who share your interests, gaining insights from peers, sharing knowledge, and staying updated on trends and technology. As AI evolves, maintaining these connections helps you stay ahead.

Why Networking is Crucial in AI

1. **Access to Opportunities**: Many AI jobs and projects aren't advertised publicly. Opportunities often come through recommendations and personal connections. According to a 2020 LinkedIn report, 85% of all jobs are filled through networking, and the AI industry is no exception.
2. **Collaboration and Learning**: The AI community is built on collaboration. By networking, you can access experts who may help you solve problems or brainstorm innovative solutions. Collaborative platforms such as GitHub and Kaggle also encourage this mindset by allowing developers and researchers to work together on projects and share insights.
3. **Mentorship and Guidance**: Mentorship is key for newcomers to AI. Networking can help you find experienced professionals

willing to guide and advise you. Many AI experts, including those at top companies like Google, Amazon, and Facebook, mentor beginners through online communities and forums.
4. **Staying Up to Date**: AI is evolving rapidly. Regularly attending conferences, meetups, and webinars is a great way to stay on top of the latest breakthroughs. Events such as NeurIPS (Conference on Neural Information Processing Systems) and the AI Expo bring together leading researchers and industry leaders to share their work, allowing you to gain insights and stay ahead.

How to Build Professional Relationships in AI

Building a network in AI requires consistent effort. Here are some ways to start:

1. **Join AI Communities:** Online communities are a fantastic way to connect with like-minded individuals. Platforms like Reddit's r/MachineLearning, LinkedIn groups, and AI-focused Slack channels allow you to participate in discussions, ask questions, and share insights. Actively engaging in these spaces helps build credibility and form meaningful connections.
2. **Attend AI Events**: AI conferences, hackathons, and meetups are fantastic spots for networking. For instance, going to events like the World Artificial Intelligence Conference (WAIC) or PyCon is a great way to soak up knowledge from industry leaders and connect with folks from top AI companies. Plus, you can jump into AI hackathons on platforms like Devpost or Major League Hacking (MLH), which is a fantastic way to gain hands-on experience and meet new friends in the field.
3. **Leverage Social Media**: Platforms like LinkedIn and Twitter are powerful tools for building an AI network. Follow AI influencers, share your thoughts on the latest AI trends, and engage with others in meaningful conversations. For example,

sharing a project you completed on LinkedIn and tagging relevant individuals or companies can attract attention from recruiters and AI experts.
4. **Reach Out for Informational Interviews**: Don't hesitate to contact AI professionals directly to ask for advice or learn more about their work. Many people are open to briefly discussing their career path or current AI projects. These informal discussions can be incredibly insightful and lead to valuable professional connections.
5. **Contribute to Open-Source Projects**: Open-source projects provide an excellent avenue to showcase your skills while working alongside others in the AI community. By contributing to projects on platforms like GitHub, you can demonstrate your abilities and collaborate with other professionals, organically expanding your network.

Real-World Example: The Power of Networking in AI

If you're curious about how machines understand human language, check out AI-focused communities on Reddit or LinkedIn. You can chat with experts and toss around your ideas. You might even bump into a researcher working on a new conversational AI project and invite you to collaborate on an open-source project. If you share your contributions on GitHub, you could catch the eye of a recruiter, opening up some job opportunities. You're making strides in your AI career by networking and showcasing your work.

THE ROLE OF CERTIFICATIONS AND ADVANCED EDUCATION IN AI CAREERS

While networking is essential, formal education and certifications remain crucial components of a successful AI career. Whether you're a self-taught developer or have a degree in a different field, obtaining certifications and advanced education can validate your skills, enhance your resume, and increase your employability.

Why Certifications Matter in AI

Certifications demonstrate that you've gained specific expertise in AI, which is especially important in such a competitive field. Here's why they matter:

1. **Prove Competence:** AI certifications show employers that you've acquired the skills to perform complex AI tasks. For example, a TensorFlow or machine learning certification validates your ability to build and deploy AI models.
2. **Industry Recognition:** Certifications from recognized institutions such as Google, Microsoft, and Stanford carry significant weight. Employers trust these credentials because they come from respected organizations with rigorous assessment processes.
3. **Stay Updated:** AI constantly evolves, and certifications help you stay current with new tools, algorithms, and technologies. Many programs focus on the latest advancements, ensuring that you remain relevant in the field.
4. **Increase Job Prospects:** A 2021 LinkedIn survey revealed that 76% of professionals felt that earning certifications helped them get hired. For those in artificial intelligence, certifications can be essential for standing out to employers.

Popular AI Certifications

Here are some of the most recognized AI certifications:

- Google Professional Machine Learning Engineer: Focuses on designing, building, and deploying machine learning models using Google Cloud services.
- Microsoft Certified: Azure AI Engineer Associate: Designed for engineers who develop and implement AI solutions using Microsoft Azure.
- Stanford University's AI Professional Certificate: One of the

most highly regarded AI programs, offering deep insights into AI theory and applications.
- Coursera's Machine Learning by Andrew Ng is a popular online course from Stanford University. Andrew Ng teaches it and provides a solid foundation in machine learning concepts.

Advanced Education: The Role of Degrees in AI

While certifications are valuable, many AI professionals pursue advanced degrees to solidify their knowledge and improve their career prospects. A degree in AI, data science, or a related field can provide:

1. **In-Depth Knowledge:** Degrees offer a comprehensive understanding of AI, covering theory, practical applications, and ethics. They also allow for specialization in robotics, computer vision, or NLP.
2. **Research Opportunities:** Advanced degrees allow participation in cutting-edge AI research, opening doors to roles in academia or R&D-focused companies like DeepMind and OpenAI.
3. **Networking and Mentorship:** Universities often have strong industry connections, giving students access to networking opportunities and mentorship from professors who are leaders in AI research.
4. **Real-World Experience:** Many programs include internships and practical projects, allowing students to apply AI concepts to real-world problems.

Balancing Certifications and Degrees

If you're wondering whether to pursue a certification or an advanced degree, it depends on your career goals:

- If you're looking to upskill or pivot into AI quickly, certifications might be the fastest and most cost-effective route.

- An advanced degree may provide the necessary depth of knowledge and experience for research, academia, or leadership careers.

The Power of Networking and Continuous Learning

In the dynamic field of AI, success isn't just about technical skills. Networking and continuous learning through certifications and education are key elements of a thriving AI career.

- Building relationships with professionals, attending AI events, and engaging in online communities can lead to exciting opportunities.
- Certifications and degrees help validate your expertise and open doors to higher-level positions.

Networking and education create a powerful combination that helps you stay competitive and grow within the AI industry. Whether you're just starting or looking to advance, remember that a successful AI career is built on continuous growth, connection, and learning.

KNOWLEDGE CHECK: CHAPTER 8

1. Which of the following is an entry-level job in AI?
   A. AI Architect
   B. Data Analyst
   C. Machine Learning Engineer with 10+ years of experience
   D. AI Ethics Consultant
2. Which skill is most valuable for transitioning into a career in AI?
   A. Graphic design
   B. Programming languages like Python
   C. Sales
   D. Public speaking
3. **True or False:** Networking with AI professionals can help you discover job opportunities and gain insights into the field.
4. **Short Answer:**

What certification or degree would be most helpful for a beginner looking to advance in AI?

9

ADVANCED BEGINNER CHALLENGES AND PROJECTS

Now that you've had a little taste of AI, it's time to jump in and explore more. This chapter will guide you through a fun journey where you'll create your AI model. You'll figure out how to work with raw data, turn it into something useful, and consider the bigger ethical picture. Let's make something you can be proud of.

ADVANCED PROJECT: CRAFTING A SIMPLE AI MODEL WITH PYTHON

Finding Your Project Focus

Think of your project's theme like the foundation of a house—everything else builds off it. Pick a theme that grabs your interest and ties into what people need. Choosing something that matters to you will keep your energy up and make the process fun. Here are some themes that could spark your interest:

- **Predictive Modeling:** Curious about forecasting future sales or predicting customer cancellations? Predictive models help

businesses anticipate trends and outcomes, allowing for more intelligent decisions.
- **Natural Language Processing (NLP):** Have you ever wondered how chatbots hold a conversation or how software analyzes if a review is glowing or critical? NLP uses sentiment analysis, tokenization, and intent recognition to teach machines to process, interpret, and respond to human language.
- **Image Classification:** Fascinated by how a computer can tell a cat from a dog in a picture? Dive into image recognition to discover the magic behind training machines to identify objects in images.

Kick things off by writing down a few topics that catch your eye, then zoom in on a practical project you can pull off. For instance, if you're into sentiment analysis, why not whip up a model that sorts tweets into positive, neutral, or negative vibes? This kind of project isn't just a learning experience—it's a great addition to your portfolio that can help you land future gigs.

Building Your First AI Model with Python

Python is super easy to use, making it an excellent choice for getting into AI. With a ton of libraries like TensorFlow, Keras, and Scikit-Learn, you can jump right into AI projects without getting lost or stressed out.

Here's how to bring your first AI model to life, step by step:

Preparing Your Data

Data is the lifeblood of any AI model, but messy data won't get you anywhere. Cleaning and organizing your dataset is essential. Here's how to do it:

- **Fill in the Gaps:** Decide whether to drop, replace, or estimate missing data points to ensure nothing disrupts your model.

- **Scale Your Data:** Standardize numbers so all features carry equal weight in the model, preventing any single variable from dominating the results.
- **Transform Text Data:** Convert text-based categories into numerical values that your model can process. For example, a column with values like Monday and Tuesday can be transformed into numerical codes.

If predicting sales, clean missing entries, scale revenue, and convert categorical data (like Weekday) into numerical values for the model.

Training Your Model

Training an AI model is like teaching a student—it picks things up from examples. So, when using Python's Keras library, you'll want to set up the model's structure: think about the layers, the neurons in each layer, and the activation functions. After that, throw in your prepped data and let the model figure out the patterns from what you give it.

Evaluating and Tweaking

After training your model, assess its performance using appropriate evaluation metrics. For classification models, use accuracy to measure the percentage of correct predictions. For regression models, metrics like mean squared error (MSE) help quantify prediction errors.

If your model overfits the training data, meaning it performs well on training but struggles with new data, consider:

- **Regularization techniques** (such as L1 or L2 regularization) to prevent excessive complexity.
- **Simplifying the model** by reducing layers or parameters.
- **Adjusting the learning rate** to improve convergence.
- **Modifying training iterations** to balance underfitting and overfitting.

Fine-tuning these factors helps create a **generalized model** that performs well on unseen data.

Making Sense of Your Results

Training a model is just the first step—understanding its results makes it valuable.

Use Python libraries like **Matplotlib** and **Seaborn** to visualize and analyze how well your model is performing.

- **Monitor Accuracy Trends:** If accuracy is high during training but drops when tested on new data, your model might be **overfitting**, meaning it has memorized the training data instead of learning general patterns.
- **Evaluate Predictions vs. Actual Outcomes:** Comparing predictions with actual values identifies errors and areas for model improvement improvement.

Example: If your model predicts sales figures, comparing its forecasts against actual revenue can highlight discrepancies and guide refinements.

INTEGRATING AI WITH VISUALIZATION TOOLS

Integrating AI with Tableau or Power BI enhances your project. These tools enable interactive dashboards that update predictions instantly. For example, you can develop a retail sales forecasting system for real-time insights into trends and inventory as new data arrives. To achieve this, establish a live data pipeline connecting your AI model to the visualization tool.

Real-World Impact

AI's transformative power isn't just theoretical—here are some real-world examples:

- **Retail:** A small boutique uses AI to predict customer demand and optimize inventory, reducing waste and boosting profits by 30%.
- **Healthcare:** A hospital deploys AI to identify patients at risk for chronic conditions, enabling proactive care and reducing emergency visits by 20%.

These examples highlight AI's practical impact and show how it delivers meaningful results across industries.

Best Practices for Effective Visualizations

Creating visualizations isn't just about making graphs—it's about telling a story. Keep these tips in mind:

- **Prioritize Simplicity:** Avoid clutter and keep visuals easy to interpret.
- **Stay Consistent:** Use a uniform color palette and formatting throughout.
- **Engage Your Audience:** Add interactive features, like sliders or filters, to let users explore the data themselves.

When showcasing your work, take your audience on a journey. Begin by describing the problem, explaining your solution, sharing findings, and concluding with key insights and takeaways. This storytelling approach makes your work memorable and relatable.

Reflecting on Your First AI Project

Completing your first AI project is significant! You've transformed raw data into a functional tool, learned AI development's intricacies, and tackled real-world challenges. Whether analyzing emotions or forecasting sales, you have impressive results. Moreover, you're primed for more exciting AI projects ahead.

TROUBLESHOOTING COMMON AI PROJECT CHALLENGES

Embarking on an AI project is like setting sail on uncharted waters—navigating algorithms, wrangling data, and exploring endless possibilities. But, like any expedition, challenges are inevitable. With the right strategies, you can turn these obstacles into stepping stones that refine your skills and improve your results.

Spotting and Tackling Common Pitfalls

The first step in overcoming challenges is recognizing them. Here are three common hurdles that can derail an AI project and how to tackle them head-on:

1. Data Quality Dilemmas
    - Imagine cooking with missing or stale ingredients—it's a recipe for disaster. In AI, your data is the key ingredient, and if it's flawed (e.g., missing values, duplicates, or biases), your model's predictions will be unreliable.
    - *Did you know?* A survey by Dimensional Research revealed that 80% of data scientists spend most of their time preparing and cleaning data. This is because high-quality data is essential for generating accurate predictions.

2. Overfitting Pitfalls
    - Overfitting occurs when your model becomes overly attached to the training data, memorizing noise and errors instead of learning general patterns. This leads to poor performance on new, unseen data.
    - Think of it like a student who memorizes answers for a practice test but struggles with questions on the actual exam. In AI, the goal is to teach models to generalize and adapt, not just memorize specific cases.

3. Integration Roadblocks

- Building a model is just the beginning; deploying it into existing systems often presents unexpected challenges. Compatibility issues, performance lags, or errors can slow progress.
- For example, integrating a customer service chatbot into an older legacy system might require additional middleware or API solutions, delaying deployment and frustrating stakeholders.

Quick Tip: Stay One Step Ahead

Awareness is your best defense. Please familiarize yourself with these potential hurdles early on so you can spot them and address them before they derail your project.

Strategies for Troubleshooting AI Projects

Cleaning and Preparing Data

Messy data leads to messy outcomes, so rigorous data cleaning is essential:

- **Fill in the Gaps:** Handle missing values using strategies like mean imputation, interpolation, or excluding incomplete entries.
  - **Eliminate Duplicates:** Remove redundant entries to avoid skewed results.
  - **Standardize and Scale:** Normalize features, such as square footage or income, so no single variable dominates the predictions.
    - *Why it matters:* Standardizing ensures that all features contribute equally to the model, preventing features with larger ranges from disproportionately influencing outcomes.

Combat Overfitting with Cross-Validation

Cross-validation is a technique that splits your data into training and validation sets, testing your model on different subsets. This ensures your model learns patterns that apply broadly, not just to the training data.

- *Pro Tip:* Cross-validation helps your model generalize better and can improve its accuracy by up to 10%, turning it from average to high-performing.

Debugging with Powerful Tools

Debugging tools are like X-rays for your model, revealing where problems occur. Libraries like TensorFlow's Debugger and PyTorch's autograd let you inspect your model layer by layer, finding inefficiencies and errors.

- *Pro Tip:* Debug early and often during development. Catching issues before deployment can save hours of frustration later.

Taking Preventative Measures

The best way to handle challenges is to prevent them in the first place. Here's how:

Thorough Project Planning

Before writing any code, map out your project's goals, select the right tools, and design your data pipeline. For example, if you're building an image recognition model, plan for preprocessing tasks like resizing images or adjusting brightness levels to create a clean, consistent dataset.

Continuous Testing

Test regularly throughout the process—from data preprocessing to model training. Iterative testing keeps your model aligned with your goals.

Stay Updated on AI Trends

AI evolves quickly, with new tools emerging. Staying informed through newsletters and forums prevents reinventing the wheel.

- *Example:* TensorFlow's 2021 update improved training speeds by 3x, significantly reducing the time required for large-scale models.

Staying current ensures you're leveraging the latest advancements.

Learning Through Setbacks

Every AI project presents challenges, but these can become valuable learning experiences.

Here's how to turn obstacles into opportunities:

- **Break It Down:** Identify the root cause of the problem—whether it's data quality, a misconfigured parameter, or an integration issue.
- **Keep a Log:** Document what worked and what didn't. Over time, this becomes a treasure trove of insights for future projects.
- **Stay Curious:** Experiment with various approaches. If a deep learning model overfits, switch to a simpler algorithm or adjust the architecture. Each attempt brings you closer to the solution.

Practical Example: Building a Sentiment Analysis Model

Let's apply these strategies to a real-world project:

Step 1: Data Collection and Cleaning

Gather product reviews, remove duplicates, and handle missing entries. Preprocess text data by removing special characters, converting to lowercase, and eliminating common stop words like the or and.

Step 2: Model Training and Evaluation

Start with a basic algorithm like Naive Bayes and use cross-validation to ensure reliability. Once the model performs well, you can explore more advanced techniques, such as neural networks, for improved accuracy.

Step 3: Debugging and Integration

Use PyTorch's autograd to debug your model layer by layer, ensuring it operates as expected. Then, it can be deployed with a user-friendly web interface where users can input reviews and instantly see sentiment predictions.

Ethical AI: A Responsibility, Not an Afterthought

As you work on your model, don't forget about ethics. Your AI is only as good as the data it learns from—if that data has biases, the results will, too. Make it a habit to check your model's output with various datasets, keep a record of your process for clarity, and always think about how your work affects society. Creating ethical AI isn't just about having the right skills; it's about making tools that contribute to a fairer and more just world.

KEEPING YOUR AI KNOWLEDGE AND SKILLS FUTURE-PROOF

In the fast-paced Artificial Intelligence (AI) world, keeping up and being flexible is like adjusting your sails to catch the changing winds. New tech and applications constantly pop up, reshaping the landscape and opening up exciting opportunities.

To stay in the loop, you need more than just the basics—you've got to embrace a mindset of continuous growth. This habit keeps your skills in demand and helps you take advantage of AI advancements to make a real difference in your work and personal life.

Exploring AI's New Frontiers

AI expands our understanding of what's possible, disrupts industries, solves previously impossible problems, and sparks new ideas. Here are two cutting-edge areas shaping AI's future:

- **Quantum Computing:** Picture a world where computers can effortlessly tackle problems in just minutes that today's supercomputers would take centuries to solve! Quantum computing is reshaping the way we process data, making a huge difference for artificial intelligence. By speeding up cryptography, enhancing climate modeling, and optimizing logistics, it's set to transform industries that depend on extensive computations.
- **Genomics and Personalized Medicine:** AI enhances healthcare by tailoring treatments. Analyzing large genetic datasets allows doctors to find the most effective patient options, reducing trial and error.

According to Global Market Insights, the AI healthcare market could exceed $34 billion by 2025, with personalized medicine leading the charge. This blend of AI and genomics is not only saving lives but also reshaping modern medical care.

These examples show that staying informed about emerging AI applications fosters intellectual curiosity and positions you to contribute meaningfully to this evolving field.

Crafting a Personal Development Plan

AI is a vast and ever-changing landscape. Developing a structured plan for learning and growth can help you navigate its complexity with focus and intention. Here's how you can build a personal roadmap:

Set Short- and Long-Term Goals

- Define where you want to go in your AI journey.

- **Short-Term Goal (6 months):** Master a specific skill, such as building machine learning models for genomic data.
- **Long-Term Goal:** Lead an AI project or publish research in your chosen niche.
- **Tip**: Well-defined goals provide both direction and a sense of accomplishment.

Identify Key Skills

Once you've set your goals, list the skills you need to achieve them.

- If your goal is healthcare AI, focus on machine learning, data analytics, and genomics.
- For robotics, delve into computer vision and sensor fusion.
- Suggested Resources:
  - LinkedIn Learning: *Python for Data Science Essential Training*
  - Coursera: *AI for Medicine Specialization* by DeepLearning.AI
  - GitHub Projects: Explore repositories like fastai/fastai for hands-on AI model implementations.

Track Your Progress

Break your goals into manageable tasks. For instance, if you aim to master Python for machine learning in three months, plan weekly objectives such as:

- Complete a specific course module.
- Develop a small project.
- Practice coding challenges
- Regular tracking keeps you motivated and ensures steady growth.

Engaging with Professional Networks and Communities

Building connections and staying active in AI communities is just as crucial as acquiring technical skills.

1. **Online Networks:** LinkedIn helps you find AI groups and connect with others in the field. Follow industry leaders, join discussions, and showcase your work to grow your network. Reddit, GitHub, and Stack Overflow are excellent for technical talks, collaborating on projects, and learning from peers and enthusiasts.
2. **Conferences and Events:** Attend AI conferences like NeurIPS or regional meetups to gain insights into cutting-edge research. Many conferences now offer virtual attendance options, making them accessible from anywhere.
3. **Hackathons and Competitions:** Join data science competitions on platforms like Kaggle to solve real-world problems, gain hands-on experience, and enhance your portfolio. These challenges, which provide practical problem-solving exposure, are also beneficial for beginners.

Staying Adaptable in a Rapidly Changing Field

Commit to lifelong learning and adaptability to thrive in AI's fast-evolving landscape.

Stay Curious

AI is a field of constant discovery. Explore the latest trends and advancements through online resources, research papers, and newsletters like *Towards Data Science* or *MIT Technology Review*.

Engage in Ethical Discussions

AI's rapid development brings ethical concerns like bias, privacy, and transparency to the forefront. Join conversations about responsible AI practices and consider how your work can contribute to building fair and equitable systems.

Start Your Own Projects

Apply your knowledge to fun projects, such as creating a chatbot, analyzing a dataset, or building a recommendation system. Please share your work on GitHub so others can explore it, provide feedback, and showcase your skills.

Leveraging Visual Content in AI Learning

Beyond coding and analysis, visuals can enhance your understanding and make sharing ideas more effective.

Ways to Use Visuals in AI Learning:

- **Infographics**: Use Canva to create diagrams illustrating neural networks or machine learning workflows.
- **Videos and Animations:** Channels like 3Blue1Brown use animations to simplify complex AI concepts.
- **Data Visualizations:** Practice creating charts and graphs with Tableau or Python's Matplotlib—these can double as portfolio pieces.

The Road Ahead

Getting the hang of AI isn't just a one-time thing—it's a journey that keeps going. If you stay curious, set clear goals, and connect with others in the community, you'll be able to keep up with this ever-changing field and really make a difference.

Remember: The best AI practitioners don't just code—they think critically, act responsibly, and embrace lifelong learning.

Your journey in AI is just beginning. Keep exploring, keep learning, and make an impact!

The Advanced Beginners Challenges can be downloaded here. Click the link or scan the QR code to download AI Essentials: Tools, Exercises & Resources.

AI Essentials: Tools, Exercises, and Resources

AI FOR BEGINNERS | 137

KNOWLEDGE CHECK: CHAPTER 9

1. **What is the first step in building an AI model?**
   A. Model training
   B. Data visualization
   C. Data preprocessing
   D. Debugging
2. **Which Python library is commonly used for AI model training?**
   A. Matplotlib
   B. TensorFlow
   C. Excel
   D. Tableau
3. **What does cross-validation help prevent?**
   A. Underfitting
   B. Overfitting
   C. Missing data
   D. Duplicate entries
4. **True or False:** Overfitting occurs when your model memorizes the training data and performs poorly on new data.
5. Short Answer:

What are two ways to handle missing data during preprocessing?

10

BONUS CHAPTER: AI AND DIGITAL AFTERLIFE

Technology is a huge part of our everyday lives. Every time we hop on social media, send a message, or surf the web, we leave behind a digital footprint. Think of it as an online shadow—constantly there but often ignored. So, what happens to all this digital information when we're no longer around? And how could AI change our digital afterlife, letting us stick around in ways we never thought possible?

WHAT HAPPENS TO OUR DIGITAL SELVES AFTER WE'RE GONE?

With the growth of digital afterlife tech, the data we leave behind can do more than sit there. It can engage, mimic our personalities, and even provide comfort to our loved ones. Companies like Eternime and HereAfter AI lead the charge, using our online interactions to create digital avatars. These avatars can chat, share memories, and help keep connections alive for those we leave behind. This chapter dives into how AI is reshaping our views on death and legacy while tackling the ethical dilemmas and cultural changes that come with it.

THE RISE OF DIGITAL AFTERLIFE: FROM MEMORIES TO AVATARS

The idea of a digital afterlife isn't exactly groundbreaking. For ages, folks have been posting photos, videos, and stories of their loved ones online to keep their memories alive. But now, AI has taken it up a notch by creating interactive digital versions of people—avatars that can chat, remember things, and even mimic a person's unique way of speaking and personality.

Take HereAfter AI, for example. It whips up digital avatars by gathering voice recordings, text messages, and social media activity. With AI, these avatars do more than just hold onto memories—they capture a person's true essence.

- **Imagine a Future Where:** You can visit a digital memorial for a loved one on a platform that hosts their avatar. With a simple voice command or typed message, you can ask questions, listen to stories, and even hear your favorite shared memories.

Ethical Questions: Ownership, Privacy, and Consent

With the benefits of digital afterlife services come questions about ethics, ownership, and privacy. Who controls a deceased person's digital data? If their digital avatar is accessible to friends and family, who decides what data is shared? Furthermore, do people have the right to dictate what happens to their digital legacy, even after death?

Key Ethical Considerations

- **Data Ownership**: Once someone passes away, their digital assets—like photos, social media posts, and emails—remain. But who has the legal right to control and access them?
    - **Privacy**: AI companies use vast amounts of personal data to create digital avatars. This raises questions about consent.

Would the person have wanted their conversations, thoughts, and messages shared in this way?
- **Impact on Grief**: Some argue that interacting with a digital avatar of a deceased loved one might hinder the natural grieving process. Instead of accepting loss, people may hold onto a digital version, blurring the line between reality and simulation.

Real-World Examples: Preserving Legacy Through AI

Example 1: *Eternime*

Eternime is a service that creates digital avatars by analyzing a person's social media posts, emails, and other online interactions. This data is then used to replicate the person's personality, allowing the digital self to continue interacting with loved ones after their death. Although still in development, Eternime is a significant step toward digital immortality, opening new possibilities for preserving personal histories.

Example 2: The MIT Media Lab's *Augmented Eternity Project*

The *Augmented Eternity Project* explores how AI can preserve the wisdom and decision-making processes of influential people. Imagine a future where you could ask for advice from an AI avatar of a renowned scientist or leader decades after they have passed. This technology allows future generations to access the expertise of these individuals, shaping the way we preserve knowledge and legacy.

Example 3: *DeepBrain AI* and Celebrity Holograms

AI-driven holograms have brought famous personalities back to life in digital form. *DeepBrain AI*, for instance, has recreated lifelike holographic performances of deceased celebrities like Michael Jackson and Tupac Shakur. These holograms analyze existing footage and recordings to recreate the celebrity's voice, movements, and stage presence, allowing them to continue inspiring audiences even after death.

THE CULTURAL SHIFT: REDEFINING DEATH, MEMORY, AND LEGACY

Traditionally, legacies were preserved through physical items such as photographs, diaries, or personal letters. However, AI and digital avatars offer an entirely new way to keep the past alive. This technology could transform how future generations remember their ancestors and how society handles the grieving process.

Cultural Considerations

- **Religion and Spirituality**: In some cultures, death is seen as a final transition, and interacting with digital versions of the deceased could be considered disrespectful or unnatural. In contrast, more tech-integrated societies might embrace digital afterlife technology as a positive way to stay connected with the past.
- **Social Media Memorials**: Platforms like Facebook already allow for memorialized profiles for deceased users. AI could eventually make it possible for people to visit these profiles and engage in simulated conversations, creating virtual spaces where the dead live in some capacity.

Visual Example

- **Imagine a Virtual Memorial Park**: A digital space where people can visit memorialized avatars of loved ones. With a simple click, they can access stories, videos, and even conversations—offering a digital sanctuary to remember and connect.

THE PSYCHOLOGICAL IMPACT: DOES DIGITAL IMMORTALITY CHANGE GRIEVING?

While digital avatars can offer comfort, they might also complicate the grieving process. Traditionally, grief follows a path toward acceptance, but maintaining a virtual relationship with a lost loved one could make it harder to let go emotionally. For some, continued interaction with a deceased individual's digital version might bring confusion, merging memory with digital simulation.

Psychological Effects to Consider:

- **Delayed Acceptance**: Prolonged exposure to a digital avatar could delay the process of accepting loss, as loved ones might become emotionally attached to the digital version.
- **Attachment to Digital Personas**: Future generations might learn about their ancestors through digital avatars rather than through memories passed down by family. This raises questions about authenticity—whether these AI versions genuinely reflect the individual as they were or if they become idealized versions over time.

As we venture into the digital afterlife, it's essential to consider the role of AI with responsibility. AI developers need to prioritize ethical standards, ensuring transparency, consent, and respect for privacy. Clear guidelines about data usage and control must be established, especially when dealing with the deceased.

Recommendations for Responsible Use

- **Transparency**: Companies should be transparent about how they use personal data to create digital avatars and allow users to control what is shared.
  - **Privacy**: It is essential to ensure that digital avatars are only accessible to those permitted by the deceased or their family.

- **Avoiding Plagiarism**: Like with any other AI tool, creating digital avatars should respect original content and aim to reflect the individual accurately without fabricating or distorting their personality.

As AI continues to evolve, digital immortality will offer new ways to interact with the past, challenging our understanding of life, death, and legacy. The possibilities are exciting and daunting, but with thoughtful and ethical use, these technologies could transform how we remember, mourn, and celebrate the lives of those we cherish.

EXPLORING THE FUTURE OF DIGITAL IMMORTALITY

With rapid technological advancements, new possibilities are emerging—some of which once seemed like pure science fiction. Concepts like neural uploading and mind preservation suggest a future where people leave behind not just memories, photos, and videos but a digital version of themselves that continues to exist after they're gone.

Through advancements in artificial intelligence (AI), brain-computer interfaces (BCIs), and virtual reality (VR), our memories, personalities, and even thought patterns could live on—creating a unique blend of the physical and digital realms.

Let's explore some of these mind-blowing advancements and what they might mean for the future!

1. **Neural Uploading:** Moving Beyond Digital Footprints
    - *What is Neural Uploading?*
        - Neural uploading, or mind uploading, is all about mapping out and recreating how our brains work—saving our minds in a digital format. Imagine keeping your thoughts, memories, and personality in a virtual space, accessible even after you're no longer around. It might sound like something out of a sci-fi movie, but researchers are seriously trying to make it happen.

Scientists aim to let our consciousness live on, even after our physical bodies are gone by figuring out how the brain is structured and how it stores memories.
- **Real-World Example:** Futurist Ray Kurzweil predicts that by the 2030s, humans may be able to upload their minds, allowing for digital immortality. However, many experts believe this technology could take several more decades to become feasible.
- **Fact:** Today, neuroscience and BCIs are advancing rapidly. Companies like Neuralink, founded by Elon Musk, are developing devices that allow the human brain to communicate with computers, bringing us closer to neural uploading.

Ethical Considerations:

While the idea of digital immortality is exciting, it also raises ethical questions. Would a digitally uploaded consciousness be considered alive? Is it a continuation of a person or just a highly sophisticated simulation? These questions bring up philosophical debates about identity, individuality, and the meaning of existence itself.

2. **AI Prediction:** Evolving Beyond Static Memories
    - *Predicting Behavior with AI*
        - Current digital avatars mainly use past data to simulate known behaviors. But what if AI could predict how someone might act in entirely new situations? With predictive AI, we might soon be able to simulate how a person would behave in the future, creating an evolving digital presence rather than a static one.
        - **Real-World Example:** Researchers have used AI to predict how historical figures like Albert Einstein might respond to modern-day scenarios by analyzing their writings and documented actions. It's almost like

asking, What would Einstein do?—and getting an answer!
- **Fact:** Today, AI is already being used to predict consumer behavior, estimate disease risks, and even anticipate criminal activity based on historical data patterns.

Applications of Predictive AI:

Predictive AI isn't just for personal use; it can also be super useful for organizations. Imagine tapping into the digital personas of past CEOs or scientists to get insights for businesses, governments, or schools. This tech could help keep the decision-making styles of influential figures alive, even after they're gone, continuing to impact society in a big way.

3. **Brain-Computer Interfaces (BCIs)**: Enhancing Memory
   - *The Power of BCIs*
     - BCIs are cool because they let your brain talk straight to computers. Initially, they were designed to help people with neurological problems control devices, but now they might let you upload your thoughts and memories into digital systems. This would be a game-changer for storing life experiences in ways we never imagined!
     - **Real-World Example:** A recent study demonstrated that BCIs allow individuals to control digital avatars with their thoughts, a breakthrough with enormous implications for preserving human consciousness.
     - **Fact:** Scientists are already using BCIs to help people with spinal cord injuries regain movement, showcasing just how powerful this technology can be.

Potential for Memory Enhancement:

BCIs could let people choose which memories to keep, share, or tweak. Imagine uploading your best memories, significant life moments, or favorite tales straight into a digital legacy that your family and friends can check out whenever they want. This tech could change how we remember and celebrate those we've lost.

4. **Immersive Memorials with VR and AR**
   - *Creating Virtual Spaces for Remembrance*
     - VR and AR have the potential to change how we experience digital memorials. Instead of just going to a gravestone, picture wandering around a virtual space that brings to life the crucial places from someone's life. You could stroll through their favorite vacation spot, listen to their voice, and relive memories like they're with you.
     - **Real-World Example**: VR platforms like *AltspaceVR* have already hosted virtual memorials, allowing friends and family to come together from anywhere in the world to remember their loved ones.
     - **Fact**: In 2023, the VR market was valued at over $20 billion. Experts predict it will grow rapidly in the next few years, leading to even more innovative uses for digital memorials.

Augmented Reality for Remembrance

With augmented reality (AR), we could soon live in a world where our loved ones can pop up in real-life spots thanks to virtual overlays. Picture this: you're in a special place, and suddenly, an AR version of a digital avatar shows up, letting you hang out and relive those memories together in real-time.

This technology could provide comfort in unique ways, making the experience of loss feel less final.

5. **Digital Immortality and Cultural Change**
   - *Adapting Rituals for the Digital Age*

- As digital immortality becomes more popular, how we think about death and mourning might change. Some cultures might embrace these new technologies to keep in touch with their loved ones, while others might consider them a bit weird and stick to their traditional ways of honoring the deceased.
- **Real-World Example:** Virtual memorials became widely used during the COVID-19 pandemic when many people had limited access to physical spaces for grieving.
- **Fact:** A 2021 survey found that 37% of Americans were interested in using digital tools like virtual reality to remember loved ones—highlighting a growing openness to integrating technology into mourning practices.

Cultural Challenges

In some cultures, death is seen as a definite goodbye. However, digital representations that can last might clash with their spiritual views or the natural way life goes. As digital immortality develops, people might have to find a way to balance technological progress with their cultural or religious beliefs about life, death, and what comes after.

6. Who Owns Your Digital Legacy?
    - *The Challenge of Consent*
        - One of the biggest questions about digital immortality is who decides what happens to a person's digital data after their death.
        - Without clear regulations, families may make decisions the deceased never agreed to, raising concerns about privacy and personal rights.
        - **Example:** Social media platforms now offer legacy features, allowing users to assign someone to manage

their accounts after death. However, these tools are still relatively new and not widely used.

- **Fact:** In 2023, over 80% of adults had no plan for managing their digital data after death, highlighting the need for better awareness and preparation for digital estate planning.

What Is Digital Estate Planning?

Digital estate planning involves deciding what happens to your online accounts and assets when you die. These services help ensure your digital legacy reflects your wishes and give you the power to determine how your online presence will continue.

PRIVACY AFTER DEATH: PROTECTING LOVED ONES

Imagine if your great-grandparents' personal stories or photos were accessible online forever. While this may sound exciting, it also raises privacy concerns.

Since AI often uses personal data to create digital avatars, mishandling this information could lead to privacy breaches, affecting the deceased and their loved ones.

- **Current Laws:** Regulations like GDPR protect personal data but often fail to address what happens after death. Governments need stronger policies to ensure AI and digital technologies respect personal data posthumously.

Should AI Create Digital Versions of Loved Ones?

AI can now generate digital personas that mimic a deceased person's personality. This means that a virtual version of someone could live on and even continue learning after they pass. But should it?

- **Ethical Concerns:** If AI evolves beyond a person's lifetime, their digital version may no longer be accurate, misrepresenting who they were. Imagine an avatar that changes over time to the point that it no longer resembles the person it was meant to preserve.
- **Solution:** Experts recommend strict guidelines to ensure digital personas remain authentic and respectful.

Who Owns Your Digital Data?

Most people have a digital footprint—email accounts, social media profiles, and photos. But what happens to these digital assets when someone passes away? There's no universal answer.

- **Legal Issues:** Some countries treat digital accounts like property that can be inherited. However, platforms often have terms of service that limit family members' access.
- **Example:** Facebook lets family members memorialize a profile, but not all platforms have such features. Clear laws are needed to help people create digital wills to ensure their assets are handled as they wish.

Virtual Cemeteries: A New Way to Remember

Virtual cemeteries allow people to visit and honor loved ones online, no matter where they are. These platforms also enable families to share messages, photos, and videos.

- Features: Platforms like Memorial Gardens or Eternal.ly let people set up virtual headstones and even chat with a digital avatar. These spaces help families who are far apart stay connected to the memories of their loved ones.

Social Media as Memorial Spaces

Social media has become a modern-day memorial ground, allowing loved ones to share memories and honor those who have passed. Platforms like Facebook offer the option to convert profiles into memorial pages, creating a dedicated space for friends and family to post tributes, share photos, and keep their loved one's digital presence alive.

- **AI-Powered Remembrance:** AI advancements enhance digital memorials. Some platforms analyze social media, messages, and recordings to create chatbots that simulate conversations with the deceased, enabling interactions based on past communications. While comforting for some, this technology raises ethical and ownership issues, as social media companies control stored data, and policy changes or deletions could erase the memories of these AI creations.

Virtual Reality Memorials

Virtual reality (VR) changes how people honor their loved ones by providing immersive experiences to visit meaningful places or attend virtual memorials. VR memorials create interactive spaces for preserving and sharing memories across generations beyond physical gravesites.

- **Example**: Platforms like Remembering. Live and GatheringUs create virtual spaces for friends and family to hold memorial ceremonies, share stories, and reflect on memories. Some VR experiences recreate a loved one's favorite places, enabling family members to revisit them. These digital memorials uniquely connect us with those we've lost, bridging distance feelings.

Augmented Reality (AR): Memories in Real Places

AR overlays digital memories onto real locations. For instance, an AR app lets you visit a park and see photos or videos of a loved one who was there there.

- Interactive Features: Some AR projects feature QR codes on gravestones, allowing visitors to see videos, photos, and tributes, merging the digital and physical worlds meaningfully.

Balancing Innovation with Responsibility

Technology transforms how we remember our loved ones, offering virtual cemeteries and VR memorials. However, these innovations raise concerns about privacy, ethics, and ownership of digital spaces. We can honor memories respectfully and meaningfully by establishing smart guidelines and using these tools responsibly.

Knowledge Check: Chapter 10

1. What is the Digital Afterlife?
   A. A virtual world where AI is used to simulate daily activities
   B. The use of AI to preserve and extend someone's digital legacy after death
   C. A video game concept involving AI
   D. AI systems used in virtual meetings
2. Which of the following is a key ethical concern regarding the Digital Afterlife?
   A. AI systems are becoming too intelligent.
     - Consent to use someone's data after their death
   B. Lack of AI in video games
   C. AI's inability to store personal data
3. **True or False:** Digital immortality allows individuals to interact with loved ones through AI-generated personas after death.
4. **Short Answer:**

Name one real-world application of AI in the Digital Afterlife.

CONCLUSION

As we wrap up this exploration of Artificial Intelligence, I hope you feel both proud of what you've learned and eager for the possibilities that lie ahead. Whether you're starting your career, looking to pivot, or simply driven by curiosity, you'll find that a solid grasp of AI basics opens doors for deeper learning.

Throughout our journey, we tackled fundamental ideas and broke down complex concepts into approachable steps. This groundwork positions you to take on more sophisticated AI systems with confidence. Beyond the technical side, we also examined the broader influence of AI—how it touches decisions, shapes industries, and intersects with ethical concerns like bias and privacy. Being aware of these issues helps ensure that AI remains beneficial and inclusive for all.

From building chatbots to experimenting with real-world applications, these hands-on exercises showed that AI is more than theory—it's a set of skills you can apply right now. But don't stop here: AI continues to evolve, revealing new challenges and opportunities all the time. Thanks to your newfound knowledge, you're equipped to stay curious, dig deeper, and keep discovering what AI can do.

Keep Learning with Your AI Toolkit

Your AI exploration doesn't end here. To help you continue growing, I've prepared a downloadable **AI Essentials: Tools, Exercises & Resources Toolkit** packed with resources:

- A handy **AI glossary** to refresh your memory on key terms
- **Hands-on exercises** for building models from scratch
- A **carefully selected list** of beginner-friendly courses to deepen your skills

Grab your copy of **AI Essentials: Tools, Exercises & Resources,** and keep refining your AI abilities.

AI Essentials: Tools, Exercises, and Resources

AI keeps changing at a fast pace, so stay flexible and curious. Join AI communities on Kaggle and GitHub, share your latest projects, and connect with others through conferences or online chats. You'll find more ways to impact this evolving field with every new insight.

Thinking about a future in AI? Whether you're drawn to data science, AI-driven healthcare, or ethical leadership, the fundamentals you've gained here can set you on a path toward exciting opportunities.

I hope this book has not only informed but also motivated you. AI can redefine industries, spark discoveries, and transform daily life. With your dedication and knowledge, I'm confident you'll play a meaningful part in that transformation.

As we wrap up, I encourage you to keep experimenting, explore further learning opportunities, and engage in the global conversations shaping AI's future. This journey is only just beginning, growing with each challenge you tackle and each question you pursue.

Thank you for allowing me to join you on this adventure into Artificial Intelligence. Here's to many more discoveries, achievements, and possibilities ahead!

Warmly,

Tina E. Bradley

Your AI Journey Isn't Over—Help Others Begin Theirs!

You've taken an incredible step into the world of Artificial Intelligence. With the skills and insights you've gained, you're ready to make an impact—and now you can help others take their first step into AI.

By sharing your experience, you're not just writing a review—you're helping someone who's eager to learn but needs a nudge to get started. Your words could inspire a future AI enthusiast to begin their own journey.

How You Can Help

1. **Share What Helped Most:** What were your most significant a-ha moments? Which parts of the book made the most difference for you?
2. **Inspire Others to Begin:** Your story could give someone else the confidence they need to dive into AI.

Leave Your Review Now!

It's quick, easy, and only takes a minute.

Scan the QR Code or Click here to leave a review to Share Your Thoughts.

Your Experience Can Inspire Others

Your review isn't just feedback—it's a powerful guide for others beginning their AI journey. By sharing your thoughts, you can help others gain the same transformative insights you did. Be the spark that sets someone on their path to success!

31-DAY JOURNEY: YOUR AI LEARNING PLAN

Weeks 1: Days 1-7 Building a Strong Foundation

Chapter 1: Building the Foundations of AI: From Basics to Key Concepts

Chapter 2: Reliable AI Resources for Beginners

Chapter 3: The Subtle Intelligence Powering Your World

Chapter 4: Utilizing AI in Your Career

Chapter 5: Staying Current with AI Trends

Weeks 2: Days 8-21 Hands-On Projects and Ethics

Chapter 6: Hands-On AI Projects

Chapter 7: Ethical AI Use and Considerations

Final Week: Days 22-31 Advanced Projects and Career Focus

Chapter 8: Career Paths in AI

Chapter 9: Advanced Beginner Challenges and Projects

ADDITIONAL RESOURCES

1. **AI Communities**: Reddit's AI Community – A forum for discussing AI news, trends, and learning resources.
2. **Scientific Papers**: arXiv.org – A free repository for AI research papers for readers who want to dive deeper into academic studies.

Foundations of AI

1. **Video**: AI Explained: How It Works – A beginner-friendly explanation of AI.
2. **Article**: What is Artificial Intelligence? – A comprehensive introduction to AI by IBM. AI Learning Resources

AI Learning Resources

1. **Website**: Coursera AI Courses – Andrew Ng's popular AI course on Coursera.
2. **Book**: *Artificial Intelligence: A Guide for Thinking Humans* by Melanie Mitchell – Great for beginners looking to explore AI from a broader perspective.

Applying AI in Daily Life

1. **Tool**: IFTTT (If This Then That) – Automate daily tasks using AI and smart devices.
2. **App**: Mint – Personal Finance – An AI-powered app that helps users manage their personal finances.

Utilizing AI in Your Career

1. **Podcast**: AI in Business – A podcast discussing real-world AI applications in various industries.
2. **Article**: How AI Can Transform Your Marketing Strategy – A Forbes article on AI in marketing.

Staying Current with AI Trends

1. **Newsletter**: Deep Learning Weekly – A newsletter with the latest trends and breakthroughs in AI.
2. **Website**: AI Conference Calendar – Find upcoming AI conferences and webinars to attend.

Hands-On AI Projects

1. **Tool**: Dialogflow – A platform for building chatbots without any coding experience.
2. **Platform**: Google Colab – A free tool for running Python AI projects in the cloud. Ethical AI Use

Ethical AI Use

1. **Article**: The Ethics of Artificial Intelligence – An in-depth look at the ethical implications of AI.
2. **Podcast**: AI Ethics Podcast – A podcast dedicated to discussing the ethical concerns surrounding AI.

Career Paths in AI

1. **Website**: AI Jobs Board – A job board for those looking to start a career in AI.
2. **Certification**: AI Certifications – Free and paid AI certifications from IBM. Advanced Beginner Challenges

Advanced Beginner Challenges

1. **Tool**: Kaggle – A platform to practice AI and machine learning by participating in coding challenges and competitions.
2. **Course**: Python for AI – A comprehensive Python course focusing on AI and machine learning.

ANSWER KEY TO KNOWLEDGE CHECK

Answers for Chapter 1:

1. **B**: ML uses data to train algorithms, while AI covers broader fields like NLP and robotics.
2. **B**: A mathematical model that mimics the human brain's neurons to process information.
3. True
4. Supervised learning involves using labeled data to train algorithms (e.g., classifying emails as spam or not spam). Unsupervised learning involves working with unlabeled data to find patterns (e.g., customer segmentation in marketing).

Answers for Chapter 2:

1. **C**: IBM SkillsBuild
2. **C**: Random videos on social media without any citations
3. True
4. Coursera and IBM SkillsBuild are two popular platforms offering free or affordable AI learning resources for beginners.

166 | ANSWER KEY TO KNOWLEDGE CHECK

Answers for Chapter 3:

1. **B**: Virtual personal assistants like Alexa or Google Home
2. **C**: AI-based budgeting apps
3. True
4. AI is used in fitness tracking apps to monitor health metrics or in diagnostic tools that provide early detection of diseases.

Answers for Chapter 4:

1. **B**: Predictive analytics to forecast customer behavior
2. **B**: AI-powered project management software
3. True
4. AI can enhance customer service by using chatbots to handle basic queries, allowing businesses to provide 24/7 support.

Answers for Chapter 5:

1. **A**: Attending AI conferences and webinars
2. **B**: Peer-reviewed scientific papers
3. True
4. **NeurIPS** (Neural Information Processing Systems) or the **AI Summit** are popular AI conferences.

Answers for Chapter 6:

1. **B**: Dialogflow
2. **B**: Recommender system
3. True
4. Key steps for building a chatbot:

Define the purpose of the chatbot. Choose a platform (e.g., Dialogflow).

Train the chatbot with predefined intents and responses. Test and deploy the chatbot.

Answers for Chapter 7:

1. **B**: AI can make biased decisions based on the data it is trained on.
2. **B**: AI systems can collect and use personal data without consent.
3. True
4. Organizations can reduce bias by ensuring their data sets are diverse and representative and by conducting regular audits of their AI systems to check for biased outcomes.

Answers for Chapter 8:

1. **B**: Data Analyst
2. **B**: Programming languages like Python
3. True
4. Certifications like IBM's AI Professional Certificate or a degree in Data Science or Artificial Intelligence would be helpful for a beginner.

Answers for Chapter 9:

1. **C:** Data preprocessing
2. **B:** TensorFlow
3. **B:** Overfitting
4. True
5. Replace missing values with estimated values or exclude rows with missing data.

Answers for Chapter 10:

ANSWER KEY TO KNOWLEDGE CHECK

1. **B**: The use of AI to preserve and extend someone's digital legacy after death
2. **B**: Consent to use someone's data after their death
3. True
4. One real-world application of AI in the Digital Afterlife is **Eternime**, which creates AI avatars that simulate conversations with a deceased person using their digital data.

REFERENCES

Adido Digital. (n.d.). *Digital eternity: How AI is reshaping life after death.* Retrieved from https://www.adido-digital.co.uk/blog/digital-eternity-how-ai-is-reshaping-life-after-death/

AI-driven solutions for enhanced plant automation productivity. (n.d.). Retrieved from https://www.plantengineering.com/articles/ai-driven-solutions-for-enhanced-plant-automation-productivity/

AI Terms Glossary: AI Terms to Know in 2024 | Moveworks | Moveworks. (n.d.). Retrieved from https://www.moveworks.com/insights/ai-terms-glossary

Amper Music. (n.d.). *Create music with AI.* Retrieved from https://www.ampermusic.com/

Anderson, J. (2023). Understanding scientific research. *Journal of Emerging AI, 14*(2), 45–56. https://doi.org/10.1000/182

Author. (2024). *How cognitive computing works* [Video]. YouTube. https://www.youtube.com/watch?v=hhIxpEfisew&t=77s

Author. (2024). *Introduction to cognitive computing* [Video]. YouTube. https://www.youtube.com/watch?v=7rs0i-9nOjo

Author. (2024). *Understanding cognitive AI* [Video]. YouTube. https://www.youtube.com/watch?v=NbcE7TmgvwA

Author. (2024). *Understanding cognitive systems* [Video]. YouTube. https://www.youtube.com/watch?v=fkIvmfqX-t0

AWS AI & ML. (n.d.). *Artificial intelligence on AWS.* Retrieved from https://aws.amazon.com/machine-learning/

Barnes, R. (2024). *The digital self: How AI is changing our relationship with memory and legacy.* Cambridge University Press.

Best AI products for the home – Quanrel. (n.d.). Retrieved from https://quanrel.com/best-ai-products-for-the-home/

BlueButterfly. (n.d.). *Virtual funerals: Online memorial services.* Retrieved from https://bluebutterfly.com/virtual-funeral

Bozkurt, A., Xiao, J., Farrow, R., Bai, J. Y. H., Nerantzi, C., Moore, S., ... Asino, T. I. (2024). The manifesto for teaching and learning in a time of generative AI: A critical collective stance to better navigate the future. https://doi.org/10.55982/openpraxis.16.4.777

Bradley, T. E. (2024). *AI for beginners: Grasp generative AI and machine learning, advance in your career, and understand the ethical implications of artificial intelligence in just 31 days— No prior experience needed.* SereneWisdom Works.

Brown, T. B., Mann, B., Ryder, N., Subbiah, M., Kaplan, J., Dhariwal, P., ... & Amodei, D. (2020). Language models are few-shot learners. In *Advances in Neural Information Processing Systems, 33,* 1877–1901.

170 | REFERENCES

Brynjolfsson, E., & McAfee, A. (2014). *The second machine age: Work, progress, and prosperity in a time of brilliant technologies.* W. W. Norton & Company.

Carnegie Mellon University. (2023). *Tom Mitchell on AI and data mining.* Retrieved from https://www.cs.cmu.edu

Clark, M. (2023). Digital democracy: How technology is shaping legacy and memory in the 21st century. Oxford University Press.

Codecademy. (n.d.). *Learn AI & Machine Learning.* Retrieved from https://www.codecademy.com

CrashCourse (YouTube Channel). (n.d.). *AI & Machine Learning playlist.* Retrieved from https://www.youtube.com/c/crashcourse

DALL-E. (n.d.). *AI-generated art & image creation by OpenAI.* Retrieved from https://openai.com/dall-e

Data Science Training Institutes in Chennai. (n.d.). Retrieved from https://freshers.jobs/data-science-training-institutes-in-chennai/

DeepBrain AI. (2024). *Virtual performances and digital legacies.* Retrieved from DeepBrain AI (DJ Saavn).

DeepMind. (n.d.). *AI research papers & discoveries.* Retrieved from https://www.deepmind.com/publications

delanceyplace archive | daily eclectic excerpts by editor Richard Vague | www.delanceyplace.com. (n.d.). https://delanceyplace.com/view-archives.php?p=2610

DjSaavn, M. (2024). *Digital legacies and the ethical boundaries of AI. Oxford Journal of Ethics and Technology.*

Domingos, P. (2023). *The master algorithm.* Basic Books.

Doshi-Velez, F., & Kim, B. (2017). Towards a rigorous science of interpretable machine learning. *Nature Machine Intelligence, 1*(2), 151–157. https://doi.org/10.1038/s42256-018-0002-3

Epitaph Memorials. (n.d.). *Personalized virtual memorials & celebration of life services.* Retrieved from https://epitaphmemorials.com

Eternime. (2024). *Create your own digital avatar.* Retrieved from Eternime (DJ Saavn).

European Commission. (2019). *Ethics guidelines for trustworthy AI.* Retrieved from https://ec.europa.eu/futurium/en/ai-alliance-consultation/guidelines

European Commission. (2020). *White paper on artificial intelligence.* Retrieved from https://ec.europa.eu/info/sites/info/files/commission-white-paper-artificial-intelligence-feb2020_en.pdf

Eubanks, V. (2018). *Automating inequality: How high-tech tools profile, police, and punish the poor.* St. Martin's Press.

Exploring the fascinating world of brain-computer interfaces—Thechipblog. (n.d.). Retrieved from https://thechipblog.com/exploring-the-fascinating-world-of-brain-computer-interfaces/

FlickerWeb. (n.d.). Retrieved from https://flickerweb.com/

Forbes. (2023). *Ginni Rometty on cognitive computing.* Retrieved from https://www.forbes.com

Gartner. (n.d.). *Understanding the Hype Cycle.* https://www.gartner.com/en/research/methodologies/gartner-hype-cycle

REFERENCES | 171

GatheringUs. (n.d.). *Virtual funeral service planning: Online memorial page.* Retrieved from https://www.gatheringus.com

GDPR. (2024). *General Data Protection Regulation (GDPR): Data privacy in the age of AI.* European Union.

GDPR.EU. (n.d.). *What is GDPR, the EU's new data protection law?* Retrieved from https://gdpr.eu/what-is-gdpr/

Google. (2018). *AI at Google: Our principles.* Retrieved from https://ai.google/principles/

Google I/O. (2023). *Sundar Pichai on AI bots.* Retrieved from https://www.blog.google

Google Magenta. (n.d.). *Magenta: Music and art generation with machine learning.* Retrieved from https://magenta.tensorflow.org/

Goodfellow, I., Bengio, Y., & Courville, A. (2016). *Deep learning.* MIT Press. https://www.deeplearningbook.org/

Goodfellow, I., Pouget-Abadie, J., Mirza, M., Xu, B., Warde-Farley, D., Ozair, S., ... & Bengio, Y. (2014). Generative adversarial nets. In *Advances in Neural Information Processing Systems, 27*, 2672–2680.

Hajian, S., Bonchi, F., & Castillo, C. (2016). Algorithmic bias: From discrimination discovery to fairness-aware data mining. In *Proceedings of the 22nd ACM SIGKDD International Conference on Knowledge Discovery and Data Mining* (pp. 2125–2126). https://doi.org/10.1145/2939672.2945386

Hindustan Times. (2023). *Sundar Pichai's bold prediction: AI to enhance professions, not replace them.* Retrieved from https://www.hindustantimes.com

Ho, J., Jain, A., & Abbeel, P. (2020). Denoising diffusion probabilistic models. *arXiv preprint,* arXiv:2006.11239.

How AI can transform education and enhance learning. (n.d.). Retrieved from https://aquariusai.ca/blog/unlocking-the-potential-how-ai-revolutionizes-education

IBM. (n.d.). *AI Fairness 360.* Retrieved from https://aif360.mybluemix.net/

IBM Quantum. (n.d.). *Introduction to quantum computing.* Retrieved from https://www.ibm.com/quantum

Imberman, S. P. (2003). Teaching neural networks using LEGO handy board robots in an artificial intelligence course. *SIGCSE Bulletin.* https://doi.org/10.1145/792548.611995

InMotion News – Tagged inventist | Guns 4 USA. (n.d.). Retrieved from https://guns4usa.com/blogs/news/tagged/inventist

int-staffing.net. (n.d.). *Top 10 jobs in artificial intelligence (AI).* Retrieved from https://intstaffing.net/top-10-jobs-in-artificial-intelligence-ai/

Jones, A., & Hernandez, M. (2022). Digital legacies: Legal and ethical considerations for the digital afterlife. *Journal of Technology and Ethics, 14*(3), 123–137.

Jones, D., & Hernandez, L. (2022). The ethics of AI memorials: Navigating privacy and ownership in the digital afterlife. *Journal of Digital Ethics, 15*(3), 220–235.

Jones, L., & White, P. (2024). *Predictive AI: Simulating behavior and decision-making beyond death.* MIT Press.

Jones, R., & Patel, S. (2024). *Spirituality in the digital age: Religion, ethics, and the digital afterlife.* Oxford University Press.

Kaggle. (n.d.). *Data science & machine learning.* Retrieved from https://www.kaggle.com

Kingma, D. P., & Welling, M. (2013). Auto-encoding variational Bayes. *arXiv preprint,* arXiv:1312.6114.

Kinfolk. (n.d.). *Augmented reality monuments for public spaces*. Retrieved from https://www.kinfolktech.org

Korshunov, P., & Marcel, S. (2018). Deepfakes: A new threat to face recognition? Assessment and detection. *arXiv preprint*, arXiv:1812.08685.

Kumar, S. (2023). Neural networks and the future of mind uploading. *Scientific American, 28*(5), 110–121.

Lee, A. (2023). Digital legacy trusts: A legal framework for the posthumous management of online data. *Harvard Law Review, 47*(6), 213–230.

Lee, S., Clark, T., & Nguyen, A. (2023). Innovations in augmented reality. *Journal of Mixed Reality, 12*(1), 33–47.

Machine Learning Mastery – Brownlee, J. (n.d.). *Machine Learning Mastery*. Retrieved from https://machinelearningmastery.com

McKinsey & Company. (2023). *The state of AI in business*. Retrieved from https://www.mckinsey.com/featured-insights/artificial-intelligence

Miller, A. (2023). Digital cemeteries: How virtual spaces are transforming grief and memorialization. *Journal of Digital Culture, 12*(4), 78–91.

MIT AI Conference. (2023). *Andrew Ng on deep learning and AI*. Retrieved from https://www.mitai.org

MIT Deep Learning Course. (2023). *Convolutional Neural Networks - MIT 6.S191 (2023)* [Video]. YouTube. https://www.youtube.com/watch?v=NmLK_WQBxB4

MIT Media Lab. (2024). *Augmented Eternity: AI-driven digital immortality*. Retrieved from MIT Media Lab (DJ Saavn).

MIT Media Lab. (2024). *Digital immortality: Preserving decision-making styles through AI*. Retrieved from https://www.media.mit.edu

MIT Technology Review. (n.d.). Retrieved from https://www.technologyreview.com/

MIT Technology Review. (2023). *Yann LeCun on convolutional neural networks*. Retrieved from https://www.technologyreview.com

Monash Lens. (2024, August 26). *An eerie digital afterlife is no longer science fiction: So how do we navigate the risks?* Retrieved from https://lens.monash.edu/%40technology/2024/08/26/1386829/an-eerie-digital-afterlife-is-no-longer-science-fiction-so-how-do-we-navigate-the-risks

Monogioudis, P. (2023). *CS 370: Introduction to Artificial Intelligence*. https://core.ac.uk/download/599240951.pdf

Moroney, L. (2024). *Introducing Convolutional Neural Networks – Machine Learning Zero to Hero (Part 3)* [Video]. YouTube. https://www.youtube.com/watch?v=x_VrgWTKkiM

Musk, E., & Hodak, V. (2024). Neuralink: Bridging the gap between brain and machine. *Neuralink Journal, 18*(3), 102–113.

NeurIPS. (2023). *Jürgen Schmidhuber on recurrent neural networks*. Retrieved from https://www.neurips.cc

News.com.au. (2024). *How the dead are being "brought back to life."* Retrieved from https://www.news.com.au/technology/innovation/inventions/ai-technology-is-bringing-the-dead-back-to-life/news-story/6979c558cc8716a75538c4d18a9e88aa

News.com.au. (n.d.). *AI technology is bringing the dead back to life*. Retrieved from https://

www.news.com.au/technology/innovation/inventions/ai-technology-is-bringing-the-dead-back-to-life/news-story/6979c558cc8716a75538c4d18a9e88aa

O'Neil, C. (2016). *Weapons of math destruction: How big data increases inequality and threatens democracy.* Crown Publishing Group.

OECD AI Policy Observatory. (n.d.). Retrieved from https://oecd.ai/en/

OpenAI. (2023). *GPT-4 technical report.* Retrieved from https://openai.com/research/gpt-4

OpenAI. (2024). *ChatGPT (October 7 version) [Large language model].* https://openai.com/chatgpt

Pan, S. J., & Yang, Q. (2010). A survey on transfer learning. *IEEE Transactions on Knowledge and Data Engineering, 22*(10), 1345–1359. https://doi.org/10.1109/TKDE.2009.191

Parker, T. (2023). Virtual memorials: How VR and AR are transforming digital legacy. *Digital Society Quarterly, 31*(2), 89–101.

Peters, J. (2024). Predictive AI and the simulation of historical figures: How AI reimagines legacy. *Harvard Review of Technology, 67*(1), 78–89.

Project December. (n.d.). Interactive AI allows people to engage with the dead. Retrieved from https://www.thesun.co.uk/news/31349764/ai-dead-husband-child-back-to-life-eternal-you/

Quantum Computing Journal. (2024). *State of the art in quantum innovation.* https://www.examplelink.org/quantumjournal

Quickinsights.org. (2024). *Exploring ridge and lasso regression in Python: Mastering regularization.* Retrieved from https://quickinsights.org/exploring-ridge-and-lasso-regression-in-python/

Ramesh, A., Pavlov, M., Goh, G., Gray, S., Voss, C., Radford, A., ... & Sutskever, I. (2021). Zero-shot text-to-image generation. *arXiv preprint,* arXiv:2102.12092.

Ramanujan, A. (2023). Reincarnation and the digital self: Hindu perspectives on digital immortality. *Indian Journal of Philosophy and Technology, 18*(2), 91–105.

Ramirez, P. (2023). Faith and the digital afterlife: Religious perspectives on AI immortality. *Harvard Divinity Review, 45*(2), 89–105.

Ramirez, T. (2024). *Digital memorials and the cultural tensions of death in a virtual age.* Cambridge University Press.

Releasit. (n.d.). *Can you customize Shopify checkout?* https://www.releas.it/sv-de/blogs/wiki/can-you-customize-shopify-checkout

Remembering.Live. (n.d.). *Virtual memorial services & tribute websites.* Retrieved from https://www.remembering.live

Roberts, A., Engel, J., Raffel, C., Hawthorne, C., & Eck, D. (2019). Magenta: A research project exploring the role of machine learning in the process of creating art and music. In *Proceedings of the International Conference on Computational Creativity (ICCC).*

Russell, S., & Norvig, P. (2020). *Artificial intelligence: A modern approach* (4th ed.). Pearson.

Scale.jobs Blog. (n.d.). Navigating the digital landscape: Top sites for learning technical skills. Retrieved from https://scale.jobs/blog/navigating-the-digital-landscape-top-sites-for-learning-technical-skills

Simplilearn. (2024). *Convolutional Neural Networks (CNNs) 101: A beginner's guide* [Video].

YouTube. https://www.youtube.com/watch?v=fPNSU4wvly0

Smith, J., & Johnson, R. (2024). Accountability in modern AI systems. *Ethics & Technology Review, 9*(2), 11–20.

Smith, L. (2023). The rise of AI in memorialization: How technology is reshaping our digital afterlife. *Digital Society Review, 9*(1), 45–58.

Smith, P. (2023). Digital assets and posthumous rights: Legal challenges in the digital era. *Yale Law Review, 92*(1), 54–79.

Szegedy, C., Vanhoucke, V., Ioffe, S., Shlens, J., & Wojna, Z. (2016). Rethinking the inception architecture for computer vision. In *Proceedings of the IEEE Conference on Computer Vision and Pattern Recognition (CVPR)* (pp. 2818–2826). https://doi.org/10.1109/CVPR.2016.308

TalkDeath. (n.d.). *Digital immortality: AI and the future of death.* Retrieved from https://talkdeath.com/digital-immortality-ai-and-the-future-of-death/

Tanaka, M., & Wilson, T. (2023). Brain-computer interfaces: Revolutionizing memory and human-computer interaction. *MIT Press.*

Technology Record. (2023). *Satya Nadella on generative AI at Microsoft Envision.* Retrieved from https://www.technologyrecord.com

TechCrunch. (n.d.). Retrieved from https://techcrunch.com/

Teachable Sorter | Coral. (n.d.). https://coral.ai/projects/teachable-sorter

TensorFlow Team. (n.d.). *TensorFlow: An open-source machine learning framework for everyone.* Retrieved from https://www.tensorflow.org

The Atlantic. (2024, July). No one is ready for digital immortality. Retrieved from https://www.theatlantic.com/technology/archive/2024/07/ai-clone-chatbot-end-of-life-planning/679297/

The AI Alignment Podcast – Future of Life Institute. (n.d.). *AI Alignment Podcast.* Retrieved from https://futureoflife.org/ai-alignment-podcast

The AI in Business Podcast – Emerj. (n.d.). *AI in Business Podcast.* Retrieved from https://emerj.com/ai-in-business-podcast

The Sun. (n.d.). *AI helps grieving families talk to their dead loved ones.* Retrieved from https://www.thesun.co.uk/news/31349764/ai-dead-husband-child-back-to-life-eternal-you/

Thompson, K. (2023). *Memory machines: AI, grief, and the digital reconstruction of the deceased.* New York University Press.

Top 10 In-Demand Tech Jobs in 2022 – Rise. (n.d.). Retrieved from https://joinrise.co/blog/top-10-tech-jobs-2022/

Tupac and Nate Dogg performing as holograms at Coachella music festival – The Verge. (2012). https://www.theverge.com/2012/4/13/2946246/coachella-tupac-nate-dogg-hologram

Unknown Author. (n.d.). *Video for beginners: Introduction to machine learning* [Video]. YouTube. https://www.youtube.com/watch?v=QzY57FaENXg

Virtual Memorial Gatherings. (n.d.). *Live streaming & tribute services.* Retrieved from https://virtualmemorialgatherings.com

What do robotics engineers do? (n.d.). Retrieved from https://www.probotcorp.com/post/what-do-robotics-engineers-do

WordPress Security 101: How to secure your website against hackers. (n.d.). https://books2read.com/b/4Agwvo

Bozkurt, A., Xiao, J., Farrow, R., Bai, J. Y. H., Nerantzi, C., Moore, S., ... Asino, T. I. (2024). The manifesto for teaching and learning in a time of generative AI: A critical collective stance to better navigate the future. https://doi.org/10.55982/openpraxis.16.4.777

Bradley, T. E. (2024). AI for beginners: Grasp generative AI and machine learning, advance in your career, and understand the ethical implications of artificial intelligence in just 31 days—No prior experience needed. SereneWisdom Works.

Brynjolfsson, E., & McAfee, A. (2014). The second machine age: Work, progress, and prosperity in a time of brilliant technologies. W. W. Norton & Company.

DjSaavn, M. (2024). Digital legacies and the ethical boundaries of AI. *Oxford Journal of Ethics and Technology.*

Domingos, P. (2023). The master algorithm. Basic Books.

Eubanks, V. (2018). Automating inequality: How high-tech tools profile, police, and punish the poor. St. Martin's Press.

European Commission. (2019). Ethics guidelines for trustworthy AI. Retrieved from https://ec.europa.eu/futurium/en/ai-alliance-consultation/guidelines

European Commission. (2020). White paper on artificial intelligence. Retrieved from https://ec.europa.eu/info/sites/info/files/commission-white-paper-artificial-intelligence-feb2020_en.pdf

Forbes. (2023). Ginni Rometty on cognitive computing. Retrieved from https://www.forbes.com

GDPR. (2024). General Data Protection Regulation (GDPR): Data privacy in the age of AI. European Union.

Google. (2018). AI at Google: Our principles. Retrieved from https://ai.google/principles/

Hindustan Times. (2023). Sundar Pichai's bold prediction: AI to enhance professions, not replace them. Retrieved from https://www.hindustantimes.com

IBM. (n.d.). AI Fairness 360. Retrieved from https://aif360.mybluemix.net/

Jones, D., & Hernandez, L. (2022). The ethics of AI memorials. *Journal of Digital Ethics, 15*(3), 220–235.

Lee, A. (2023). Digital legacy trusts: A legal framework for the posthumous management of online data. *Harvard Law Review, 47*(6), 213–230.

MIT Technology Review. (2023). Yann LeCun on convolutional neural networks. Retrieved from https://www.technologyreview.com

NeurIPS. (2023). Jürgen Schmidhuber on recurrent neural networks. Retrieved from https://www.neurips.cc

O'Neil, C. (2016). Weapons of math destruction: How big data increases inequality and threatens democracy. Crown Publishing Group.

OpenAI. (2023). GPT-4 technical report. Retrieved from https://openai.com/research/gpt-4

Roberts, A., Engel, J., Raffel, C., Hawthorne, C., & Eck, D. (2019). Magenta: A research project exploring AI in music. Proceedings of the International Conference on Computational Creativity (ICCC).

Russell, S., & Norvig, P. (2020). *Artificial intelligence: A modern approach* (4th ed.). Pearson.

Smith, P. (2023). Digital assets and posthumous rights: Legal challenges in the digital era. *Yale Law Review, 92*(1), 54–79.

TensorFlow Team. (n.d.). TensorFlow: An open-source machine learning framework for everyone. Retrieved from https://www.tensorflow.org

Technology Record. (2023). Satya Nadella on generative AI at Microsoft Envision. Retrieved from https://www.technologyrecord.com

Yang, Y.-H., & Lerch, A. (2020). Music and artificial intelligence. In E. Miranda (Ed.), *Handbook of artificial intelligence for music* (pp. 153–182). Springer. https://doi.org/10.1007/978-3-030-18250-9_6

Printed in Great Britain
by Amazon